The Journey to Healing:

Love,

Yourself

Elizabeth A. Miles

Ladybug Press
PHILADELPHIA, PA

Elizabeth Miles/Ladybug Press
Cover Design: Elizabeth A. Miles
Editor: Joshua Stuart

Book Layout © 2020 BookDesignTemplates.com

The Journey to Heal: Love, Yourself/ Elizabeth Miles. -- 1st ed.
ISBN 978-1-7332829-3-2

Dedication

To Jessica, Andrew, Abigail, and Mary: Truly, I have the best kids in the entire world, and for that I am eternally grateful. I love you all so much! Thank you for your love, support, and for continuing to believe in me.

To Jake and Stacie: I could not have done it without the two of you coming into my life, and standing with me, side-by-side, through the struggle. I am so grateful for you both, and that you have become part of our family.

To you, the reader: This is dedicated to you. May you always find a way back to yourself, and know that, no matter what, everything will always turn out okay.

Contents

Introduction

DEAR SELF,

I feel such an intense and profound emptiness within. I am empty. Depleted.

My body, my mind, and my spirit have been ripped open leaving me raw and exposed. My heart has been torn out.

The pieces of me, of my life, of my existence, are scattered all around me.

One by one I pick them up. Piece by piece I put them back together.

Today is another day!

Today is the day that I choose me.

Love,
    Yourself

Dear Reader,

We can look at the pain we feel like a wildfire.

It ignites as a small campfire. It can get very hot, uncomfortable, and unmanageable very quickly. We do what we can to control it, manage it, and extinguish it. We are holding on tight for survival. Eventually, just when we think that fire has gone out, a gust of wind comes along, reigniting that fire. This time it's more powerful and dangerous. It's difficult to maintain. That wildfire can grow big enough to destroy the entire forest.

Here's the thing about wildfires: even though they might have burnt down that forest, we have to remember that the trees will grow back. They are not lost forever. When they do, they come back stronger, healthier, more beautiful. The fire was the catalyst to bring this more enduring, lush, healthier forest to life...

...but that does not mean we would welcome that fire back into the forest ever again.

There is no free pass from the obstacles that life throws at us. They begin like that campfire, and might even become seemingly unmanageable, like the wildfire. We are going to experience pain. It's important to remember, though, that we, too, will come back stronger, more powerful, more aware, healthier, and more vibrant than before.

You survived! It is your time to rebuild. Do not look back at where you were. That's like sending an invitation for the fire to return. That wildfire killed you once. Let it teach you the lessons it needed to teach you, but keep it in your past, so that you can continue through life on the new journey that is unfolding before you, feeling empowered, confident, and free!

Love is from the heart; a gift we give to ourselves first, and then to others. Appreciate all that YOU are, so that you can truly appreciate that of another. Letting go of all that does not serve you or your highest good requires honesty and total surrender, along with the willingness and determination to create space in your life to make room for the joy, peace, and happiness that life is all about. This takes forgiveness, compassion, and understanding—not without fear, regardless of it.

This is an act of loving yourself!

The moment you surrender and love yourself so completely that you are willing to choose yourself--*your* voice, *your* dreams, *your* meaning for success--is also the moment when you put your faith and trust in the Universe. Here is the moment when magic can truly start to happen in your life. You will have realized that the power lives within you to choose and create something greater for yourself. It's a beautiful place to wake up each day, and the place where true freedom and limitless possibilities can flourish. Because when you are loving yourself, you can accept your dreams as having potential, and you are willing to put forth the effort to make them a reality. From that place of self-love, you accept who you are, and allow others to share in your authenticity, too.

But...

There can be no forward motion without healing and forgiveness. Take a step back, let go, and cut away all that once was. Though painful, this is only for a moment in time. Then, there is the space and sense of peace that allows us to shape and mold life into everything our hearts desire. Let go! Heal! Live from a place of love, not resistance, fear, or desperation. Love yourself!

Give yourself permission to take this journey. Permission to forgive. Permission to let go. Permission to open your heart and find love for yourself. By doing so, you open yourself up to a new world of possibilities. Receive the magical abundance this Universe offers. This is your time!

By reading this book, may you find peace. May you find forgiveness. May you find compassion. May you find joy. May you feel the love for yourself, and within yourself, that you truly deserve.

Love yourself!

Grace and peace,

Elizabeth

CHAPTER 1

The Journey Begins

WE ARE ON A MOUNTAIN in life. In the climb, it's a challenge. You test your strength and your physical limits. When the climb gets unbearable, we hit a peak. It's time to release it. The descent, that journey back to safety, is the path of healing. It's a cycle, constantly moving, ebbing and flowing. Sometimes we are moving between different mountains at the same time. Relationships. Career. Finances. Self-doubt. These are all mountains we face.

Life gets complicated. We hurt others. We feel pain and hurt *by* others. Sometimes we hurt them again in return, and it becomes a seemingly never-ending cycle of struggle. I choose to believe that life is happening for us, though. The mountains we climb are our lessons, unfolding for us to improve, to learn, and to grow. This means that we do not have to stay stuck in the pain, hurt, and sadness that unfolds. Instead, we heal! By allowing ourselves to heal from that pain, we can free up our time, energy, and imagination to create the beautiful life we truly want to live.

But *how?*

Some might see the healing process as the release point; a moment when you let go and release the wound. One might argue that this is a totally acceptable means of getting over it; essentially saying, "let's just forget it even happened" and move on. Have you ever had a situation occur when you were hurt, but decided not to say anything? Or decided only to talk about *some* of the ways it impacted you?

I know I have!

It's easy to think that this is the better way. We don't want to be in pain. We do not want others to be in pain. We want others to think highly of us as individuals, to love us. We are afraid of what will happen if we use our voice and express ourselves fully and completely. Or maybe we don't quite know how, so we'd rather not do it at all.

It is important to remember that only dealing with part of the situation does nothing to benefit either person involved. This is not true healing. This is covering things up with a band-aid, almost like taking the shortcut through the mountain. Except the scar is still there.

When you are climbing a mountain, not fully dealing with the situation leaves you working so hard, you find yourself spending so much time, energy, and resources trying to convince yourself that you are "fine". It becomes easy to look in places outside of yourself to get you to where you want to be. It leaves you thirsty, never satisfied.

True healing begins the minute after one *chooses,* decides, to fully release the pain; to actually let it go, so that it no longer impacts our thoughts, feelings, or emotions. Healing is not just about one specific situation. It is about understanding the emotions and patterns that lead up to that situation, forgiving, letting them go, and then making another choice for how we want to fill that space.

It is a process that begins with choice! How do we want to heal? How long will the process take? The decision, making a choice to heal, creates this space where possibilities can emerge. It creates awareness. There is so much power there. You have made the choice to love yourself!

And then the journey can begin.

Do you want to call in more positivity? Change? A rebirth? Or, maybe you want to heal from identifying as a victim; bitter and angry. Holding a grudge is always an option. But if you are carrying that with you, are you truly healed? Do you want to welcome back more of what you had before? Stop and think about that for a minute.

You get to choose!

Healing is a time for creation. You are the artist, crafting the scenery for how you want your life to look. Where do you begin?

I encourage you to start here. Within the pages of this book, you will find tools, and hopefully, words of encouragement, to help you through the healing process. Each chapter is based on a different topic related to healing. At the start of each chapter, you will find a letter, or several, reflecting some of the emotions that might be presenting as you move through life. Think of these as love letters to your soul. You can choose to take them at face value—the introduction to each section. Or, you can use them as templates to write your own letters to yourself. At the end of the book, I have some reflection questions that you can use to guide your healing process, and I have started a few love letters that you can finish on your own.

Remember: You are never stuck. You are never lost. You are never alone. You always have the option to choose to love yourself enough to let go of the things—people, places, situations, feelings—that do not serve you well in your life.

You are a powerful force of creation and creativity. You have the power to let go! Are you ready? Love yourself enough to move through this book and consider what is presented. I hope this serves you well.

If you are visiting with me again, well, a lot has happened since we parted ways at the mountain. But for our newcomers, I will recap a few things:

- A troubled marriage
- Limiting beliefs
- Time was ticking away
- Was left feeling stuck, lost, and alone.
- Chose to make a few big pivots in life
- MUST live life now!

Since then, a lot has changed. I have come to a deeper level of self-awareness, a better understanding of how I need and want to show up, what was holding me back, and (for those of you who asked) who my husband truly was. And most importantly, I had to ask myself the hardest question ever asked: why? But none of that could have happened if I had not allowed myself permission to start to see a tiny spark of light within myself.

I believe I mentioned that, at the conclusion of book one, my (now-ex-) husband and I were still figuring out our mess. In the end, figuring it out meant that I had to come to terms with the emotional abuse he put me and my children through. I also had to come to terms with the fact that I allowed it. That was difficult, but once I could see both of these, I recognized the situation for what it was—with the awareness that this one, big, giant lesson was needed to push me to stand on my own two feet and live what I truly felt was a purposeful life. Once I realized it and challenged him, and challenged myself, calling him out on more of the lies, the BS, the pretending, and calling myself out on the reasons why I was choosing to continue listening to it; well, let's just say things did not end with ice cream cones and unicorns.

It was ugly.

Going through it, I could never quite see the other side of the mountain. I always wondered what things would look like on the other side but didn't ever believe it would or could be okay. But, guess what? It IS all okay! I overcame the struggles. While some of the details will be shared later in these pages, life goes on.

Life goes on!

And, no matter the pain or hardship you might find yourself dealing with in this moment, **you can overcome it, too.**

In truth, though, there was a moment when I seriously considered rewriting *This Is Where You Pivot.* I questioned whether the book would be valid, relevant, and as helpful as I intended it to be as it was written, particularly as events continued to unfold. Then, I realized that some stories are just meant for a sequel, a part two. The first book helped me to share my story and got me to a place where I could recognize, accept, and lean in to wanting more out of life. This second act, however, is about the aftermath of that.

Then I realized that this is how life unfolds. One long series of chapters or novels crafted into what becomes our own individual journey. We get to choose the cast of characters and control the setting, tone, and message. While we cannot go back and change situations that occur, we can rewrite the story from the moment we choose to pivot towards something different for ourselves.

If you are finding yourself in a place where are thinking "what the hell just happened to me and my life?"—know that you are not alone. I have been there, too. As I was sitting in the shit of my own storm, wondering, "why did this happen to me, and where do I turn next?" I had to find a way to pull myself out.

It might not feel it right now, but I promise that you can overcome it, too. You can do this, no matter what "this" looks like. But first, you must love yourself enough to let it all be okay. No matter what!

I also spent some time thinking about the word "shift," and realized that there's a reason why my first book was "the shift" from fear to freedom. That shift began on the mountain. That was the start of it all, the pivot, a point of no return. When I wrote it, my husband and I really were figuring things out. More importantly, I was figuring ME out. I was starting to understand that I was tolerating what was happening from a place of fear, and that I held myself in such low esteem that I allowed myself to believe I did not deserve better. Making the choice to change that was the first pivot, shifting my mindset to the possibility that maybe, just maybe I was worthy of living a great life.

So, like I said, it is all okay. Life goes on. However, once you are fully awake, there is no going back to sleep.

Once you are awakened, you see all the synchronicities in the Universe and all the possibilities for your life. You understand the power you hold within you and can see the magic that you are truly able to create for your life. The best part is—you now realize that you deserve it. Even if you don't fully believe that you deserve it yet, you can see the potential, that it's well within your reach, and you are no longer willing to stay on the path that you have been walking.

You are never stuck. You are never lost. You are never alone.

Things have evolved a little (well, a lot) since we parted ways in …*Pivot*. For this reason, I need and want to re-introduce myself to you and the world…

Hello! My name is Elizabeth Miles. I am an author, life coach, and healer. I am also on a mission to empower YOU to take control of your life, to open your heart, take charge of your fear, and step into the life you were born to love.

You might be wondering— "born to love? Don't you mean born to live?"

Nope. I want you to live the life you were born to LOVE.

If you are reading this, you are a sentient being. You are already living and breathing. You were born to live. That does not mean that you love the life you are living. I want you to love the life you live. When you wake up every single day, I want you to love your body, love your mind, love your relationships, love your job. Wake up, stretch, and be excited for what that day will bring you, because you are loving life. And even if you wake up in a bad mood one day (because, let's face it, as I said – life goes one), or you get stuck in traffic, or just having one of "those" days, you can still tackle the day with the understanding that it's all going to work out, that you can make it through, and that you will do what you can to soothe your soul when needed.

So, again, live the life you were born to love.

I know. Sounds so romantic, over-the-top, and dreamy. Maybe you are thinking "no way possible." Or maybe you are shaking your head wondering "how the heck do I get there? I can't just leap from where I am right now over to where I want to be."

It is not easy to just leap. Or, is it?

Every step, no matter how big or small, towards that dream life changes your reality. There is an energy shift within you, and you start to attract more and more of what you want. Like attracts like. You are shifting your vibration.

When you pivot and make the conscious choice to move towards new results for yourself, you shift your perspective. That dream is no longer a far-off, or never-going-to-happen wish. Your eyes turn and focus on the vision, and you take a step in the direction of what you want. With each step, the rest of your body starts to follow. Before you know it, you are well on your way to your new life. Eventually you get to a point where the scale has tipped. There is no going back.

Along the way, there might be a few stumbling blocks. Those are things that either need to be removed from your life, or things you need to heal from—not just smooth over and ignore. You will want to tackle these head on, not just push them aside. Shoving the bumps out of the way takes a lot of energy. They are likely to return in some capacity somewhere down the line. The lessons will keep showing up until we learn them. So I encourage you, when the lessons show up, recognize them as lessons, and then use all of your strength and determination to truly "get" the meaning. We are here to learn and grow, so stay open to the knowledge that the Universe is bringing forward for you.

For me, my bumps in the road hit me on the head every single time another affair popped up for my ex-husband, or every time there was an issue with money. Every fight with a family member or with someone I thought was a friend. Every time I felt a deep depression or had another health issue. I was constantly being triggered by people, places, events, and situations, and it left me feeling a lot of anxiety, sadness, fear, depression, and chronic physical pain. I was not learning the lessons.

Once I started making some connections between how I was feeling and how I was allocating my energetic resources, a lightbulb went on for me. I realized that, for me to get where I wanted to go, I first had to get rid of the baggage that was holding me back. I had to allow myself to heal. First, I had to allow myself to recognize that I was worthy of healing. I had to love myself.

I had a lot to heal from: from my marriage as well as my childhood, perceived failures, setbacks. I was scared at first, but over time, as I started to let things go, the process got a bit easier.

Spoiler alert—this is not fun but is definitely worth it. When you open yourself up to healing, you start to make connections about your life, and you can begin to put the pieces together to find your ultimate purpose. Through healing, you discover who you truly are, what you are made of, and what you are capable of.

You have something amazing to offer the world. We need you! We need your creativity. Use your gifts and talents; use your mind, your body, and your soul to share your dreams with us.

But first, the healing. Why?

Well, if you are holding onto the negativity, sadness, and fear there is likely a feeling that you are not worthy of the abundance this life has to offer you. When that lack of worth is present, you will try to create, but it will be from a place of lack, from a place of fear, not from a place of love.

The healing process is a journey to understanding yourself and the world around you. You embrace the fear within you. You embrace the pain, the sadness, and allow yourself to sit with it while you open your heart to understanding what it has brought you. When you do this, you open yourself up to receive greater love, joy, peace, happiness, and abundance. Healing gives you the strength, courage, and confidence to move forward on whatever mission you have in life, with the understanding that there will be bumps in the road. Sometimes things won't work out the way we want or intend them, but when you allow yourself to heal, you are able to see those unexpected outcomes from the perspective of learning and growth, rather than failure, doom, and gloom.

Let's get started...

First, love yourself!

CHAPTER 2

Play and Creation

DEAR SELF,

What is it? What is that "thing" that your soul is longing to create? What gift do you want to leave with the world? You have so many gifts and talents. There are so many possibilities. You have a voice. How will you use it to create a force for goodness? For joy? For connection? For celebration?

Think about this on your journey. What are you creating in your thoughts, words, actions, and dreams?

Love,
   Yourself

DO YOU REMEMBER RAKING UP THE FALL LEAVES only to jump right in when you were done? Do you remember the feeling of the cool, crisp autumn air on your skin, or the bright hues of orange, red, and yellow in the leaves? Do you remember that beautiful, melodic crunch of the leaves as you then started picking up that pile of leaves, handfuls at a time, and throwing them around, just so you could do it all over again?

This is a world of whimsy, at the intersection of Peace and Playful. It's magical and it's what alignment feels like. You find yourself in this moment, once you have healed through the struggle and the pain, accepted, let go, and found forgiveness. After that release, once it is all over, you are in this beautiful space; this energy that allows you to take in all the beauty and joy and glory this world has to offer. You are in flow and it feels amazing. Fear is no longer welcome here.

From this flow state you can finally appreciate the wonders of the world. There is happiness and bliss. In this space, you show up, and can create authentically, freely, as you choose to. Your creation is totally and uniquely you. You are authentically aligned with your passion and purpose.

Sounds great, right? Except getting there is not always a smooth and easy road. For me, this moment usually happens just after something big goes down. When I say big, I mean things like: a rough day at the office; an argument with a loved one; missing a meeting; that feeling of anger that comes over me when I am triggered, only to then realize, I was just afraid. Sometimes I know it is happening when I wake up and feel so run down that it seems as though I cannot possibly be a grown-up that day. Sometimes it happens after having a negative thought about myself or remembering a point in my life that was painful or sad.

Some days are just like that.

There is a trigger there, a reason why it brings me out of that flow.

This is the point where healing can begin...

...and then play and creation can occur.

This morning, on my way to the local coffee shop, I found myself walking down the street, crunching in the leaves, noticing their bright and beautiful color. Vibrant. Fall is a time when the Universe is preparing to rest, to hibernate through winter, yet I could not help but marvel at how alive these leaves appeared. There I was, at forty, kicking the leaves around, crunching and playing. I gave myself permission to be a child again. Laughing. Smiling. I, too, finally, for the first time in a long time, felt alive once again. And I realized...

...I missed me!

See, in the middle of the chaos, I forgot who I was. There came a point when someone asked me the question ..." what kind of music do you like?" ... A simple question, I know, but I did not have an answer. I knew I liked music, but I spent a long time listening to what other people wanted to hear, and accepting it as my favorite, that I forgot what I liked, and that it was okay for me to like those things. The moment I realized I could not answer, I got chills. It was a pivotal moment for me, realizing I had lived far too long in the wrong reality. I did not know who I was, or what I stood for. My vision for my life was so severely blurred, and the version of me who desperately wanted to laugh, play, and have fun, got lost.

Coming to this moment, this realization, happened after the shit show. I had to climb the mountain. I wish that had not been the case, but it is true. I had to go through the struggle. Then, seemingly out of nowhere, a moment of clarity occurred.

What do you long to create in this world? How do you want to show up? I encourage and implore you—do the work. Forgive. Release. Let go. Heal your heart. Heal your mind. Heal your spirit. So that you can set yourself free to play and create the life that you want – a life that feels good to you, and in which you wake up every single day feeling inspired and excited to live. Remember who you truly are and love the you that you be!

While you might have a dream you long to achieve, the road to get there lies in your ability to love yourself enough to go along for the journey. Your soul is already at the finish line. Are you able to love yourself enough to feel the essence of how truly good and capable you are, and then allow yourself to stand up and move?

If you do not have a specific dream but wake up feeling sad and unfulfilled, that, too, is a sign that something needs to shift. Is there stress around family relationships? Money? Do you struggle to find time to just sit back, relax, and decompress from the hustle and bustle of everyday life? Life is meant to be enjoyed. Can you love yourself enough to help yourself figure out why there is such discontent?

Please say yes. Even if you do not believe it, right now, just say yes. Pivot. Shift. Move. Making a decision *is* an action step. That choice alone is an empowering one. It means you are ready to stand up for yourself and for your life.

Life is a challenge. What I have come to realize is, it does not have to be a competition. You can explore life, experiences, seek knowledge, just to explore. There does not need to be mastery involved. It is okay to be the student and to continue seeking knowledge just for the fun of it. It is okay to play. Play with the concept of who you are to figure out who you want to be. You do not have to have *the answer* immediately.

I did not know this when I was growing up. Here I was at forty, alone, playing in the leaves outside of a coffee shop on a street in Chestnut Hill. Finally, I understood that I could sit back, breathe, and take in new experiences for the enjoyment of it alone. That gave me hope. I did not have to live with such pressure.

When I was a child, I did not know what I wanted to be. As a teenager, I still could not figure it out. Everyone around me said, "hey, you are smart, you are going to do big things with your life." When you are thirteen, this is a set up. What big things? How does one define "big?" How are you supposed to know when you are that young and inexperienced at life?

To me, I thought that if I found financial success and love straight out of college, I succeeded. End of story. If I didn't, I succeed at letting other people down. When I was told I needed to make something of my life, I had no idea what that could, or should be, but I understood, very clearly, that the expectation was high. I took those expectations to heart, and then continued trying to fill shoes that I did not want to be wearing.

I was forty years old before anyone asked me what I thought, honestly, about a topic or situation. I was scared as hell to answer. I realized that, before that time, I had big ideas, big dreams, and goals that I was not allowing myself to express. In truth, I *wanted* to make something of myself, and had a general framework for what that looked like, but I was living like that did not matter. I accepted everyone else's framework as my own.

Until I was ready to stand up for myself, regardless of whether anyone else wanted to stand with me or not, they would remain a dream. The reason: I was too afraid of trying it on my own. For the longest time, most of my life, I believed I needed to rely on other people to help me get where I wanted to be. More specifically, that I needed them to either: validate that what I wanted was okay, or to hand me the easiest, quickest path to get there.

I believed I needed someone else to hire me for a job. I believed I needed someone else to validate my goals. I believed I needed people and things to make me feel better. I believed I needed someone else to tell me how to live.

27

When I started baking as a kid, everyone around me told me I was amazing at it. Many said, "you should open a restaurant." I just sat back and said "okay" and that became my focus. Nobody asked me what I really wanted. Nobody explained that I could take some time to explore the possibilities, to get so lost in the learning that I could truly choose whatever it was that I wanted that "thing" to be that I succeeded at. Thus, began my cycle through life, trying to compete my way to the top, always trying to learn a job or skill as fast as I could, even if it meant taking short cuts. I competed with myself to see how fast I could go. I competed with those around me to see how fast I could promote out of a position. It was never about enjoying the process. Instead, it was always a matter of trying to succeed and make something of myself because someone else told me that was what I was supposed to do. I did not want to feel the pain of failing. I was afraid that if I failed, those around me would think I was bad and then leave.

The entire time, though, it never *had* to be a competition.

Challenge. That's a different story.

Every single time I was put in a situation that required me to try something new, guess what? If it was not something that I aced from the first attempt, I ran from it. I kept telling myself things like: It is too hard, or... I can't do it. Or, I would blame the system and tell myself that it was someone else's fault. I was so uncomfortable with trying, failing, and trying again, that I avoided any situation that required mastering a new skill. I did not want other people to think I was bad, or wrong, for not knowing.

What I also eventually realized: I accepted the finish line that other people handed me, as well as the path that they dictated, without challenging myself to push past it, or to find another way. I adopted other people's definitions of success, and whenever I could not "succeed" fast enough, I gave up. When I did get to that finish line, I stopped, instead of challenging myself to see how far I could run.

What I did not realize – those were moments to play and explore. To try something new and decide if it was for me, or not. To go on a curious adventure and see who I could be once I mastered something.

Life should always be a challenge—not a struggle, but with just enough resistance to make you uncomfortable. Then you take action and move. This is how you grow. Set your sights on the level ahead of you, and then push yourself a little harder in order to reach it. Then push a little more still so that you can pass it.

If it is a challenge for you, good! See it as a good sign that you are on the right track. Because here is where you get to play and explore the inner workings of you!

In the workplace, eventually, you become the leader that pushes those behind you to work harder to catch you. It's a beautiful cycle that allows everyone to show up, as they are, be the best that they can in this moment, and then choose whether they want to push harder in order to grow or stay where they are in the pack. It really is a choice.

Always allow yourself time and space to play. Never stop working hard to grow.

Love yourself!

CHAPTER 3

No More Hiding

DEAR YOU,

Why do you feel so afraid? What makes you want to run and hide? What caused you to run? Why not stay and fight? Why did you shut down?

Now is the time that I get to decide what happens next. Do I hide? Continue to take more abuse? Continue to let the world kick me when I am down? Or do I rise up and show the world who I am, and what I am made of?

I know I am strong. I know I am capable. I know what I have been able to accomplish on my own up until now. Maybe it's time to share that with the world.

How do I find my voice? What do I want to tell the world? I think I need to start with myself.

Love,

Yourself

HAVE YOU EVER WANTED TO HIDE? Are you hiding right now? That's the face of fear, rearing its ugly head. What are you afraid of?

Fear begins within yourself, the ego. Maybe you fear that you are not good enough. There is a lot of self-doubt and constant self-judgement. From there, because we don't believe we are worthy, we feel the need to defend our actions, and we fear that others will leave, or judge us for our actions. We begin to fear new experiences. Instead of life being one joyous, miraculous adventure, it becomes ridden with fear. And we go into hiding, hoping that one day that fear will go away. Fear gets us lost in this nasty cycle, constantly creating more things to be afraid of.

So what's the solution? How do we stop the perpetual cycle of fear, stop feeling so paralyzed, and start to feel motivated and empowered enough to take the next steps forward?

There is no easy fix to this. It's painful, and we are wired to avoid pain at all cost. We have to go back to the beginning and tell ourselves, our younger selves, that we are safe; that we are worthy; that we are enough. The more you tell yourself this, the more you begin to believe it. You get to choose that for yourself, recognizing that you are not the same person you were back then. You have grown, changed, learned, evolved.

Maybe right now you don't feel truly worthy. Tell yourself that you are, every single day! Cheat the fear out of its power to keep you stuck where you are.

For me, I took myself back to when I was five years old. Two key moments occurred, making me feel so alone, small, and afraid. These are the moments that shaped my belief that the world wasn't safe, and that I needed to run away and hide.

The first was a sunny and hot summer day in the city. I am watching my little self, at five years old, being bullied, again, by some kids in the neighborhood. At that time, I believed they were going to hurt me. Their words were so mean and hurtful; hateful even. Did they not realize how powerful those words were or how much of an impact they would have on me? Their words hit me like a bullet going through my heart. It took me a very long time to understand how big the impact was.

The second moment took me to my bedroom, and a painful experience that I blocked for so long. Growing up, I had dreams that hinted to this moment, but they came in fragments that took a long time to piece together. I finally heard the words that had been locked away for so long – "what feels good isn't bad...I will have my way with you...nobody is going to believe you...nobody likes a tattletale...if you say anything, I will tell them you are lying and nobody believes a kid..." When I met that moment, when the complete picture of what happened came flooding back, I was overcome with anger, resentment, panic, and the intense urge to run and hide.

I sat down with my younger self on the concrete pad outside of our house. I could see the tears rolling down the face of my younger self, and once again, I could feel the pain of those moments. These were such pivotal experiences in my young life. With the hot sun beaming, the energy settled down. At that moment, it was calm, and all we could hear on that big city street was the sound of a few birds chirping in a tree. I take a deep breath and tell that little person sitting in front of me, my little self, "Love yourself!"

She looks up at me with scared, confused five-year-old eyes. She is just a little girl, and has already felt so much emotion, pain, judgement. Some of it from herself, which she does not understand. Some of it from other people, which she also does not understand. This statement, while short and simple and sweet, was not something that was taught to me at a young age.

I say to her...

"What happened was wrong. They were mean. Hurtful. Disrespectful. They were being bullies. That is not okay. But that behavior—what they said to you—that is not who you are! It is not a reflection of you at all. I know it scares you but know that you are safe!

One thing that you do not know is that there is energy all around you, as well as within you. You can access it and feel it. That means that you absorb the feelings of other people—good, bad, happy, sad, scared, and all other emotions on the spectrum of feelings that exist in the Universe. You feel the pain that these people have caused you right now. It is real. It is valid. That is okay. Understand, though, that you also are feeling *their* fear and sadness. They must be in pain for them to be so hurtful towards you and anyone else.

It does not make what they did right. It does not make it okay. But what that does mean is that it is not you, and it is not yours. You do not need to hold on to their stuff. What they did or said does not make you bad or wrong. You are beautiful. You are smart. You are creative. Funny. You have a heart of gold. And you have an amazing life in front of you.

Do not shrink down and hide. If you do that, then they win— they succeed in making you feel small. Do not give them that much power over you.

I know it feels scary and that you feel that you are all alone. You feel that you are too small to defend yourself, or to stand up for yourself. You are a big heart in a little body. You have big things to say to the world. Important things. If you let these guys make you believe that you need to run and hide, then you will not be able to express yourself to the world.

You are not alone. I know it seems that the people in your life right now are not there for you. I am going to tell you a little secret, though. You cannot see them, but you have a whole team of guides and angels around you, watching over you, ready to help you whenever you need assistance. Call on them for guidance and support. Call them when you feel alone or afraid. They are there, and they will never let you fall. They will never let anything happen to you that you cannot overcome. They know how strong your heart is.

Do not run. Do not hide. Don't let them stop you from being happy and free."

After my little heart-to-heart with my younger self, I pick her up and give her the biggest hug and whisper in her tiny year "I am so proud of you."

With tears rolling down both of our faces, the scene fades away, and my current self feels a little lighter, free.

It's an interesting thing about hiding...you can be physically present, making it *seem* as though you are there, but really, energetically, you are somewhere else. I did this my entire life. I hid behind other people, wanting them to be my voice. I hid behind other careers, not believing I could do the work I wanted to do. I hid behind relationships, too afraid to stand up for myself and block out the toxicity coming at me from those around me. That left me feeling very stuck and isolated. I didn't see, feel, or believe that I could make decisions for my life, and by hiding, I was not allowing me to be myself. I didn't want to be hurt. I didn't want to be judged. I didn't want to be seen. Staying back in the shadows, for a long time, was easier than standing up and being noticed.

As a student—I was too afraid to speak up in the classroom. I sat in the back every chance I got. I didn't raise my hand to participate unless classroom participation was a requirement. I didn't allow myself to ask questions because I was too afraid the question would sound dumb.

As an employee—I was too afraid to go for the jobs that I felt I really deserved, and when I did get into a position that I liked, I never followed through to continue moving up the ranks. I got bored and left before that could happen. I rationalized this by telling myself that the opportunities were not there, or the company just was not the right fit. I always blamed it on the corporate culture, when really, I was afraid to show myself what I could do. I was afraid of the failure that I knew would come because of needing to learn new skills. I thought I had to be perfect at everything. When things came easy, I stuck to them. When things were not, I ran.

As a mother—I was afraid of letting my kids down. I knew what I saw and felt as a kid. I did not want my kids to go through that. I tried to overcompensate, then undercompensate, trying to find the right balance of nurturing them, loving them, and teaching them about accountability and consequences. When my kids were younger, I had this old-fashioned idea about love and what it meant to be a family. I didn't understand what being a mother was truly all about, except loving your kids, and making sure that they were clothed, fed, and went to school. I always had a sense of fear as a mom. That stemmed from my own insecurities, not feeling like I was good enough, smart enough, loving them enough to raise them to be wonderful human beings and contributors to society. What I also came to realize is that, for the longest time, I didn't love myself enough to be the example they needed me to be.

Living in all this fear led to living by going through the motions. I woke up, showed up, and did what I had to do to get by, but never truly showing up and acting as I felt I should. I was hiding. I didn't want to make waves, be different, stand out, or stand up and make a scene, and I avoided conflict at any and all costs. I said "yes" to everything, so as not to upset the person making a request. I felt the disappointment from saying "no" more than they ever did. I believed that by saying "no" I would somehow shatter their world completely. Looking back, I realize how that might sound arrogant, or elitist, but in the moment, I felt far from elite. I didn't want to say "no" because I didn't want to disappoint them and give them a reason to leave. I'll call that perpetual people-pleasing syndrome. I had to give up a lot of myself to make everyone around me happy, because I was scared of being alone.

It is uncomfortable to face fear. Painful. Overwhelming. I was afraid that I was insignificant, showing up small when I had big visions for how I wanted to help the world. Looking back at the situations that took place was hard. But in order to heal it, you have to feel it. Then you can truly let it go.

The opposite of fear is love. While there is no true antidote for fear, the more we embrace loving ourselves, as we are, where we are, and for who we are in this moment, the more control we gain over fear.

So, how about you? How is fear showing up for you, and from what are you hiding?

If you aren't sure, I encourage you to explore this. Fear is going to show up time and time again as you make the changes to up-level your life. It takes time to learn how it manifests for you. It's different for everyone. Tune into your body. Tune into your thoughts. Do this on a regular basis. Eventually, you will start to understand what your "true" voice sounds like, what it feels like, versus the voice of fear. When you start hearing yourself saying things like, "I might be crazy for wanting that; there's no way that can happen," or "who are you to want that," or you feel a heaviness come upon you that drags you down and makes you feel off, that might possibly be fear coming for a visit, and you need to take action immediately to stop it from holding you back.

Here's the thing: it's difficult to create big change, for yourself or for anyone else, when you are standing in the background, not allowing yourself to be noticed. And it's difficult to move into the forefront of your life if you are constantly allowing fear to paralyze you. Once I realized that by making new choices, I would no longer feel stuck, and that by making a new move would alleviate the feeling of isolation, I felt empowered. Then, one step, one moment at a time, I had to create new habits for myself so that I would no longer remain in hiding. This did not come natural to me at first. I had to face my demons—those fears of being teased and laughed at. This was not a fast change. It truly was a process.

Where and how did I start?

By creating a vision for my life, and a why so compelling that I had no other alternative but to come out of hiding and be seen by the world. All the "I want" and "I wish" had to become "must" and "should."

I wanted to help people. I wanted to make a positive impact on the world. I knew that my story, while very similar to so many others, could be brought forth so that others could see that they are not alone, and that, no matter how sad things look, there is always hope.

Until that moment comes when you have truly given up, anything and everything is possible if you are open to the possibilities. I wanted to create a new and better life for my family, erase that "money is not grown on trees" mentality and the "we aren't rich" mindset that left my parents in a panic every week, wondering if they were going to be able to put food on the table, and that left me struggling to find that feeling of safety and security in my own bank account for the longest time. I wanted my kids to know that abundance, happiness, and love, is available to everyone, including them. There was no magic ticket or path to receive them. It simply came down to a matter of choice. If, I chose it, and loved myself enough to believe that I could have it, I could then start to move myself towards the things I wanted. I wanted to set the example so that the kids knew that if they chose it for themselves, they could do that, too. I wanted them to feel the safety and security that I grew up hoping for, and I also wanted them to know that no obstacle or situation is too great for them to create something new or different for themselves.

Things I wanted to say to myself (and believe):

- It was never your fault.
- You can't control other people.
- I am proud of you.
- Yes, you can! And, yes, you should!
- You are amazing. You are strong. You are beautiful.
- You are smart, talented.
- You matter.
- Forgive yourself. Forgive those who did not value you enough to honor you.
- You are not stuck. You are not lost. You are not alone.

Eventually, I got there. But, it's a process. Contrary to what we want to tell ourselves, there is no easy road to healing or self-love. The opportunity to choose these is always present, but once that choice is made, we embark on a journey with no set itinerary or schedule. It unfolds as we need it, and as we allow it.

I saw that the world could look different. I saw that my family could look different. I felt in my heart of hearts that I had the ability to be part of the change. Once I saw it, I could no longer hide in a business that was meant for someone else. I could no longer hide behind the excuses of "there's not enough time," "there's not enough money," or "I don't know how to do this." And, I could no longer hide in a marriage that had me questioning my worth, my ability to love, and my ability to show up in the world as a decent human being, on a daily basis.

The question of "why" is so critical in the healing process. It gets the ball rolling. Question anything and everything, all the time. When you ask "why," you will get an answer in one way or another. When I was first asked "why," it was by a business coach shortly after I opened my bakery.

A simple question: "Liz, why do you do what you do?"

As soon as she asked me the question, my body went cold.

I gave her the answer I thought she wanted to hear "because I like to bake and I am good at it."

Guess what? That wasn't the answer.

That call put me in such an uncomfortable place, and I will never forget the profound impact it had on my life. She kept asking me "why" and every single time, I got more and more uncomfortable. Eventually, I got a little defensive because I felt she was challenging me for what I wanted. It was triggering me and that feeling of not being good enough. I got upset, angry even.

Forty minutes later, after she continued to press the "why" issue, I hung up from our call confused, and almost in a daze. For years, I thought I knew why I did what I did, but was beginning to realize that my reasons and intentions were very much flawed in focus. As an entrepreneur, that was not going to cut it to launch and grow a profitable, sustainable business. My "why" had to be bigger than me, and beyond the scope of trying to make people like me. Building a business just to prove yourself and your worth in the world is not a good idea. With enough determination, yes, it can make you money, but that does not mean you are fulfilled.

Once I started to further question "why" and really search for the honest-to-goodness answers (not the ones I thought were correct, or I thought people wanted), I was opening myself up to the possibility of healing, change, and growth. I could now question my heart, my pain, how I was using my energy, and the resources I needed to show up in the world.

Here's the thing: if it feels uncomfortable to ask, keep asking. There is a reason why you feel so unsettled. Explore that! Be ready for answers and new awareness to come through. From this space, you get to understand so much more about yourself.

Stop hiding from yourself!

Ask why. Be open to the answers. Create new possibilities. Love yourself!

CHAPTER 4

Love and Loss

DEAR SELF,

While I realize it needed to be done, I wish it could have been different. Enough is enough. Enough struggle. Enough hurt. Enough pain. I am done feeling alone. I have lived in such a state of sadness, hoping the storm would end, and, eventually, a rainbow would appear. But the storm tormented me long enough. I am done. I am exhausted. Drained. Now is my time. Time to heal.

Love,
    Yourself

DEAR YOU,

Today is a new day! You are beautiful. You are brave. You are courageous. You are freedom, hope, joy, and success. You are a light for the world.

Love,
    Yourself

THE DAY MY EX-HUSBAND CAME FOR HIS STUFF, a day I was dreading, and thought would be the hardest day of my life, was a pivotal one. For a few minutes it was sad, hard, and painful. Then, when I remembered the lies that he told me. I remembered how he swore he loved me and wanted to be with me, while simultaneously planning secret meetings with the other women he was seeing on the side. I remembered the lies he told our kids.

I asked myself "why are you holding on so tightly to *this*?"

All the fights! All the times I was told it was all in my head. The times I ended up at the emergency room, and my kids telling me they were afraid of him, too. All those nights crying myself to sleep. One-sided conversations. Broken promises.

Again: why was I holding on?

He had been out of the house for a few weeks by that point. So, I then realized that in the time he had been gone, all of those pains in my stomach were no longer there. They had been there the entire time that I was with him. I was able to relax in the time since he'd been gone. I was sleeping better. I lost weight. I was finding it easier and easier to take care of my health. I got up to go to the gym. I was more productive at the things I wanted to do with my life. The house was not only quiet, it was peaceful.

Why again was I so scared and nervous about this day? What exactly was I afraid of?

I had this breath of fresh air come over me. I could breathe. Everything lifted away. The house seemed brighter, lighter. The energy changed completely, and I knew everything was okay.

It had been weeks since I spoke with him, or even saw him. Knowing he was out there in the world was hard at first, but soon, that sadness dissipated. I was laughing again, playing and enjoying life. I knew good things were coming for me.

They already had. I was free.

I didn't have to hide behind the lies. No longer did I have to make everything seem normal and okay—for myself, for the kids, for him, or for anyone looking in. Up until this point, I didn't want those on the outside to see the pain that I was in. I was the girl that everyone thought had it all together. And he let the world believe he was such a great dad and loving, loyal husband. I couldn't let anyone see the dark, harsh reality.

When I got married, I promised to love, honor, cherish, in sickness and health, till death do us part. I took those vows seriously. Sadly, he did not. That was his choice. But I should never have had to hide. I always felt that I had to be a certain person— that certain mother and wife. I don't leave my family in times of crisis. I stay and fight for my family. That's what I was supposed to do, right? That was my choice!

I hid my face for so long. Forgetting who I was. That playful girl, who loved to have fun, who had a huge heart and loved people and the world around her. Where did she go?

On that day, even though the divorce papers had not yet been signed, I was free. For the first time in almost twenty years, I felt like I could step out into the world and be confident in who I was. I felt confident in myself. In my ability to lead. To love. To laugh. But it had been a twenty-year cycle of pain, sadness, anger, and frustration. That doesn't just go away the second he drives off in the moving truck, and by that point, my body felt so used to being in a constant state of anger and frustration. How do you let that go? How do you heal a broken heart?

I had good days, and then bad days. Then really terrible days. I would think to myself, "well, you did it. You lost him. You lost yourself. You lost your family. You lost your way."

I felt directionless. Powerless. Scared to make another mistake. Scared to take a step in any direction. Fear had found me once again! I kept making more excuses, bringing more pain, and feeling more heartache. I felt so trapped in my life, in my mind, in my body, in this relationship that I knew was over. Why did I fear losing someone and something that wasn't really what I wanted in the first place? I felt as though I was grasping at straws. Some days I thought I had it all figured out. Turned out, I knew nothing whatsoever. I was trying to be someone and something, but really, I didn't really know what or who that was. And for the longest time I sure as hell did not believe I deserved anything more.

He would cheat on me, then lie about it, then manipulate me into believing it was my fault. He told me I was crazy. He told me I was the abusive one. Whenever I would ask "why did you lie to me?" the response was always "I don't know" but he never wanted to figure it out—only pretend to try. Or he'd say, "I didn't do anything wrong; this is all on you." He kept telling me "I love you, and I want to be with you" and "I am sorry and I won't do it again."

He continued living the life he wanted, trying to make me believe everything could and would be okay. I believed the lie, creating the illusion that he was a decent man, a supportive husband, a loving father. I kept telling myself that he was doing the best he could. Ironically, while I was trying hard to keep people out of the mess, so many people saw him for who he was. They knew. They saw the manipulation. The lies. The cheating. They knew that, if he was really trying to make things work, he would have done something to change—like maybe choosing and committing to no more affairs or choosing to continue in therapy to understand himself more. Heck, he could even have decided to leave.

Instead, he told me I was crazy. Through every argument, every time I showed any level of distrust, every time I kicked him out and then took him back, he told me I was the abuser and that I had to change. Even though he told the women he was sleeping with that I was crazy, that I was a bad wife and a bad mother, that I killed myself and left him alone to raise his kids, that I was fat and ugly, somehow, *I* was abusing *him*. He took every single negative thing that I ever thought about myself and used it against me.

Eventually, he told me he was sick, and was getting worse. He claimed his mental health was declining but chose to let it fester. He did not get help. Instead, he told me he wanted to kill me and rape me. He told me he wished I were dead and should have left me long ago.

Then why did he choose to stay? And why did I choose to let him? Because while he was telling me it would all be okay, at the time, I heard that coming out of his mouth as "I will help you be okay" - instead of realizing that I needed to make it okay for myself.

I ended up in physical, mental, and emotional pain. I landed myself in the psychiatric unit at the hospital for contemplating suicide—twice. I went to therapy. Attended classes. Read every book on personal development that I thought would help. Hired a coach. I knew I had to change. I showed up to do the work. To get better. To heal myself. To question "why am I doing this?" I thought he was trying too, but this was part of the illusion he wanted me to believe. The truth is—HE abused ME. Not the other way around.

I was phrasing the question completely wrong. Instead of asking it in terms of "why am I hurting him like this?" I should have been asking "why do I keep hurting myself like this?" The truth is—he never changed, though he wanted me to believe he did, or would, or wanted to. He was living the life *he wanted* to live. Why was I not allowing myself to live the life that I wanted to live for myself?

When I allowed myself to be brutally honest with myself, I came to realize just how little I was valuing myself. I did not love myself enough to see that I deserved better, even though I knew exactly what I would be saying to my BFF if she was in this same situation. I would tell her to love herself enough to let him go, and that life on the other side of it was way better.

Just as I had to go back and have a talk with my younger self, I had to let the healing begin, letting out the anger and frustration I felt towards him. I couldn't pick up the phone and call him to do this. In truth, that would not have been beneficial to either of us, and this process was not about him anyway. This is an important point to remember: your healing journey is about YOU, and you alone. The same holds true for your path to self-love. You do it for you and you alone.

I spent a lot of time journaling letters to him. They went something like this…

"The last time you cheated on me was the LAST time. The final act of deception. Because I will no longer stand to be treated with such disrespect. If you wanted to leave, if I was so horrible to you all this time, you could have gone, and left on your own. You are responsible for your own actions. Eventually, you pushed too far. You thought you could get away with it, but you pushed me to the point of no return. Now you are gone, and you blame me.

Here I sit, wondering "why?" I am left here to pick up the pieces, for myself and for our kids. What was the point? What was there to gain? How could you have done this? Are there really people out there so cruel and heartless? And was I really that naïve to let and keep you in my life for so long? Why?

Why does it hurt so bad to know that you are out there and not caring? To know that you are sick and won't help yourself. Why does it hurt to know that we can't help you either? Why does it hurt to think about you out there with another woman? Why do I still believe I love you? Or that my life can't get better unless I work on this with you?

I allowed you to put me through hell, to put our kids through hell. Now, you have left, and are out there in the world, to create a new story for yourself, telling the world how you are the victim.

We know who you are! We know the truth. We survived you.

For that, we are stronger. We overcame it. We are left here, together, to strengthen our connection, without you! Still asking "why" but asking in order to understand the lessons we can learn, so that we never make the same mistake again.

We, too, get to start a new story, without you. We survived! And now we are free!"

And just as I gave myself time to feel through the anger and pain towards him, I had to keep reminding myself of a few things, too...

"You will never make this same mistake again. You are stronger now, wiser. It's time to move on. To realize how strong you are and rebuild. You can do this! You are capable.

He was only holding you back. He's going to talk badly about you. He's going to hop into another relationship quickly. The truth is—and you know this, he already has. Every single time he told you he was done with the cheating; he still was actively engaged with many other women.

This was not about you. EVER. It was never your fault, and you could have never prevented it. This was not because of any shortcoming of you. How someone else chooses to behave is a direct connection to how they feel about themselves. Sadly, when they show up and treat us poorly, we are in the line of fire. The good news: you get to choose how you respond to the situation.

Rebuild. Reconnect with yourself. With your kids. Rediscover who you are.

You are worth so much more than he could ever give you. Go out there and change the world. Show the world that there is life on the other side. That starting over is a chance to live. Because it is, and you deserve it. You were abused, yes, but you do not need to stay a victim forever. You get to choose!"

I had to keep that one in a place where I could read it over and over again. Eventually, I started to feel it in a way that gave me hope and inspiration, instead of pain and sadness. There were days when I felt inspired, happy, and strong, but there were also days when I wanted to stay in bed, hide under my blanket, and cry. The journey to heal a broken heart is not a linear one. Know that you are going to have good days, and bad. Over time, the number of bad days get less and less, or less severe. The good news is, that along the way, you are also learning new tools and strategies, and you are finding out just how great of a person you are. The more you find love in your heart for yourself, the easier things become.

Heartbreak is the stuff that all good romantic comedies are made of, right? We all want to fall in love. We all want that "special someone" to come into our lives and make us feel whole and complete.

I don't know about you, but when I was a little girl, I had this vision for my dream guy. I knew what he looked and sounded like. He was going to be my Prince Charming, riding in on his white horse, whisking me away from the sadness and pain that was happening in my house growing up. We were going to have 2.5 kids and live in this gorgeous house that always seemed to clean itself. And he would love me for me. That guy would see me, my true me, and love me anyway. And we would live happily ever after.

Except that "the end" came before I ever got happily ever after. Well, sort of...

I grew up without a sense of self-worth. I didn't feel pretty. I didn't feel confident. I didn't have any self-respect. No concept of boundaries. I didn't realize that I was valuable. I looked for external sources of validation to prove my worth. That external source being my ex-husband. I didn't believe that I was complete without a man. I believed that I needed a "mister" to show the world that I was worth something, valuable. Someone desired to spend their life with me; therefore, I must be okay.

These days, I find myself in reflection. How frequently do we allow ourselves that moment to sit back and remember our own, individual past? How often do we honor our journey, who we once were on the path to where we sit right now?

51

I don't think we talk about that enough.

If you are anything like me, when you hit that pivot point, that moment when we realize it's time to do something different, you take that project head on, in a relentless pursuit to change - as fast as humanly possible. It becomes easy to forget that change, development, growth, takes time. We lose sight of the past, focusing solely on the path ahead of us. It also becomes easy to forget that who we were, as we sat in the shit of our own storm, mattered to our purpose.

The minute we decide to change, we want to forget everything else we knew. As soon as I woke up to the reality of the pain that I was sitting in, I remember feeling like I was stuck swimming underwater, kicking as hard and fast as possible to get myself up to the surface to breathe. I couldn't think about the past. It hurt too damn much. I was angry. I was scared. I was confused. I felt lost. All I could do was focus on the steps in front of me and try to figure out how to navigate life in the new, fresh air.

Let me take you back to one of those days for a minute...

I was sitting in my car, staring at the judge's signature on the paperwork, thinking, "what did I just do?" I just signed my fate. I was holding a temporary protection from abuse order against my husband. In a short while, he would be served his copy, evicted from our home, and gone from our lives. I was panicking. There was a piece of me that felt this tremendous weight had been lifted off of my shoulders, yes. But within minutes of driving away from the courthouse, I had to pull over. I couldn't hold back the tears anymore. The entire time in the courthouse, I told myself, "stay strong, this is what you have to do. You are doing the right thing for yourself and for your kids."

By this point, I had told my story so many times to multiple people—the police, the court assistant helping me file my case, the judge, the people in the women's center. I was exhausted. And I couldn't stay strong for one more second.

I could almost feel the anger he was about to experience when the sheriff showed up to deliver the news. I didn't know how he would respond, and that terrified me. Would he try to come after me? Would he try to take my kids away? Was he going to take this as a wake-up call and get himself the help he needed? Would he be okay?

I also sat in fear, realizing that I was now responsible for myself and the kids. On my own. What the heck was I going to do? I got married right after college. How would I take care of myself? How would I take care of them? How could I make sure that I was okay enough for myself and for them? That terrified me.

In that moment, with all the questions running around in my mind, and the tears streaming down my face, there was still a hope lingering inside of me that, somehow, we could make this work. I still wanted my family to be okay. I hoped that he would someday understand.

That day, I felt stuck. I felt lost. I felt alone. That was uncomfortable, and I wanted to do everything I could to avoid feeling it.

Here I am, months later. As I look back at the days and weeks just after, I recognize that I went right into survival mode. I dove headfirst into healing, for myself and my kids. That meant therapy, coaching, a lot of alone time with my journal. In the beginning I wanted to make the healing about looking ahead, forgetting the past and just looking and planning for the future. It has been a layered process, to say the least. Just when I thought I was doing okay, something else would pop up, some memory, a random image or comment, and I kept seeing there was more to heal from.

Eventually, I hit a brick wall. The wound seemed to refuse to want to close. The more I tried to tape it up and pour super glue over it, the more it wanted to open. I thought I was over the anger. Thought I had gotten past the pain, and believed I was in a good place emotionally, physically, and spiritually. Then, one day, I was sitting in meditation, and I heard the words, "return to your heart." I went cold inside and out. An image of my ex appeared in my visual field, and all I could think was, "well, shit...I didn't see this coming."

At this point, I am very in-touch with my spiritual guides. When I get that icy-cold feeling inside, I know that's my intuition trying to tell me something. I immediately ask, "what is going on?"

Then I listen for an answer.

At this moment, the answer didn't make sense. It took me to my wedding album. It took me to a box of old photos from when the kids were little. I sat on the floor of my room, again, sobbing, and remembering where my heart had been for so long. I spent so much time running away from the past, trying to reinvent myself and my life, trying to be strong, trying to hold it together, trying to heal, and trying to start over, that I totally forgot that, at the core of who I was, I was love. I am my heart.

Feel it to heal it! I knew I had to let a few feelings bubble up so that they could release out. In my case, during that time, I thought I needed to overcome the anger, so I let myself feel it, and that became my initial focus. I thought that, through that, I would find the self-love that I had been lacking.

I tried to tell myself for so long that he never loved me. I looked back at my time in that relationship and felt guilty for spending time with someone who didn't truly want to commit his life to me or to our kids. I tried to use that as a path to healing. That somehow, since he was never in love with me, it would make the cleaning-up and moving-on of my life that much easier. Except I was forgetting one critical piece of the puzzle...

My love for him was real.

It was easy to say he didn't love me. I tried to run away from the pain by being angry at him. I spent time building myself up to the point that I could feel love for myself. I finally knew, felt, and understood my worth, and what I was capable of. Except that my love for him was real. Regardless of the choices he made for himself, I forgot to acknowledge that I loved him, with my whole heart and soul, to the point that I allowed myself to lose myself. I allowed myself to turn away from my own heart, from knowing who I truly am. I allowed myself, on multiple occasions, to almost die, for him. Whether it was healthy or not, my love for him was real. I had to remember that and allow myself to grieve the loss of that love.

At the core of my being, I know my heart. I know I am love. That I came from love. That I choose to radiate love into the world. No matter what storm I am walking through, I will always be love. I had to honor my past to remind myself of that.

What I came through, that was no easy feat. I see that. I see how strong I had to be in order to do it. I also see that I don't have to run away from that person I once was and go screaming headfirst into the person I want to be, forgetting the old version even existed. Just because we remember where we came from, doesn't mean we have to go back. I can remember my past and look to the lessons the situation provided. I can honor who I was and find compassion for myself and those involved. I can thank the situation for helping me become who I am today. And I can do that, continuing to walk forward.

In that, I find freedom. For that, I am grateful. With that, I still choose love.

In the beginning, when the ex came along and started showing me attention and telling me how great he thought I was, it was attractive to me. It didn't matter that he didn't mean a single word of it. I believed him. He said it, it must be true. That's at least what I wanted to believe and wanted to prove to the world, even though I saw the red flags.

This happened because I didn't honor and respect myself enough…I did not love myself enough (or at all) …to see the value in what I could bring or was bringing into the world. Don't let this be you, too!

The experience led me to really question what it meant to love someone. Does it mean I have to give up my own identity in order to make them happy? What do I sacrifice for love? Does loving someone mean that they come first? Does unconditional love mean they get to do whatever they want, and we stay together because of the whole "till death do us part" thing? Or, does loving someone mean lifting them up and inspiring them to be a better version of themselves, encouraging them to go after their dreams and being there on the sidelines, cheering them on to victory?

How do you love?

For me, my story should have gone a little more like this…

Growing up, I knew my worth and respected myself enough to know that I could trust that little voice inside my head that was telling me he was not exactly being truthful. I would have had enough confidence to set and uphold boundaries, so that, when he showed me who he truly was with the first affair, or the first threat, I would have known then to leave. I wouldn't have spent the next twenty years trying to force a relationship that never should have happened in the first place.

But I didn't love myself. I believed I deserved it. Believed I could change him. I believed that if I pushed hard enough, eventually the scales would tip and he would then have to love me unconditionally and truly, because I put all this time, effort, and energy into making myself a better person. That didn't happen. At first, the more I tried to better myself, the angrier and more resentful I got with myself because he wasn't really changing. I thought I was doing it wrong. I thought that there must have been something wrong with my methods of self-improvement.

Except there wasn't.

What was wrong was my skewed view of myself. When you don't love yourself, you tolerate anything. When you don't love yourself, your standards are low and you take the first offer that comes your way, instead of waiting for the opportunity that you truly want. When you don't love yourself, it becomes easier to make excuses for decisions that other people make.

In truth, going through all of the heartache and loss made me a stronger person. I came to find myself. I improved myself enough to know that I was okay. There was still a lot to process and heal from, but I loved myself enough to know that I was going to be okay.

How do you recover from a broken heart? How do you recover from that sad feeling of grief that sits within your heart after the loss of a loved one (no matter the capacity)?

Choose to heal.

It's time to go within. Heal yourself—mind, body and soul. When you do, you also help those around you to heal as well. But, please, do not do it all for them. Start by doing the work for **you** first. Their healing, and their overall lift in vibration, will ultimately happen as a result of you doing what you need to do to take care of yourself. Allow yourself to feel the pain. Don't bury it down. Let it flow up and out of you. Meditate. Journal. Cry if you have to. Phone a friend who can listen without judgement, or without responding. Call a friend and say, "I need to talk, but can you please just listen...you don't have to say anything." Advocate for what you need. Don't be afraid to ask.

In order to love another, truly and completely, you have to love yourself completely first. Growing up, I thought it was wrong to say that I loved myself. If I did say that, it meant that I was prideful, boastful, arrogant. Through the healing process, I realized that nothing could be further from the truth. There is a big difference between loving myself enough to stand up for myself and being so "in love" with myself that I make everyone else around me feel small and unworthy. When you love yourself, you can also see the inherent good in the people around you, so arrogance is never an issue. When you love yourself, you take pride in your work, but can celebrate it for yourself without needing to have the entire office patting you on the back for a job well done.

And you know what? That feels so much better than trying to prove my worth to the world.

You are a shining light! Give yourself permission.

Love yourself!

CHAPTER 5

A Vision for Yourself

DEAR SELF,

What happened to you was not your fault, but staying a victim holds you back. When you play it safe, you know what to expect, and you feel dead inside. You are playing small. And when you play small, THEY win. When you choose to shine, YOU win!

Love,
    Yourself

DEAR YOU,

How do you see yourself?

How do you talk to yourself?

Forget what other people might think. Truly, their opinion does not matter. You are priceless, and if they don't see or feel your value, then they are not the people for you.

Love,
Yourself

THE KIDS AROUND ME DIDN'T ACCEPT ME as I was growing up. Neither did my family. I was different. I felt so much loneliness and isolation. That led me to bad relationship after bad relationship. The longer this went on, the lonelier and more isolated I felt.

I had no direction. I drifted from job to job. College educated, but never really knowing what I wanted to do or why. I felt isolated. Afraid. Unsafe.

How would I keep myself alive or put food on the table? I didn't know how. Nobody showed me what to do. I was screaming to find people, a purpose. Something, or someone, with whom I could feel safe. I wanted someone to take care of me.

What I finally came to realize is—I was always capable of caring for myself. My purpose is, and always has been, to be me. To show up in the world and be unapologetically me—a light of hope for those around me. A smile of warmth and compassion. Just me. Nothing more. Nothing less. Nothing to control or change—about myself or anyone else.

Me.

In terms of finding my tribe, what I eventually understood was—I always had this guidance system—a team of guides and angels around me, providing guidance, safety, security. All I had to do was tap into this. They were, and always had been, my tribe. One that would never judge me, lie to me, hurt me, or abandon me. To access it, all I had to do was tap into myself; go within. Let go of control, then surrender and trust.

I was safe. I was secure. I was protected. I had been the entire time.

I found myself at the library not that long ago, with a stack of books in my arms. As I walked down the aisle to find a table, one book seemed to jump off the shelf at me. It was a book that talked about narcissistic abuse, sitting on the wrong shelf, on the wrong side of the library entirely. I knew this was a sign. There was something here for me.

For those who have experience with it, you will recognize the symptoms. For those who might be new to the term, those who could possibly be diagnosed as a "narcissist" feel entitled to anything and everything and have an exaggerated sense of importance. They exaggerate the achievements, talents, and circumstances surrounding their life. Perhaps you have met someone who likes to take advantage of others, or who seems preoccupied with power, and behave in an often arrogant, boastful manner, and seem unwilling or incapable of accepting feedback or criticism from others.

Okay, so that describes some of the traits of a narcissist, but what makes the narcissist abusive? In my case, my ex-husband was the master of deceit, lying to me about anything and everything he could think of, including his whereabouts, those he was spending time with, as well as his persistent, ongoing extramarital affairs. To make it worse, I knew every single time he was cheating on me, but he would gaslight me, intentionally making me distrust my intuition because I had no proof of his actions. I distinctly remember several instances of him telling me directly "it's all in your head; you can't prove it." And he always found a way to criticize me, both to my face, to those around me, and to the women he was cheating on me with. In the midst of this, he would still find a way to look me in the eye and tell me how much he loved me and wanted to be with me. Every single time another affair was revealed, he assured me he had no idea why he was behaving this way and would, without a doubt, stop.

There was financial sabotage, his fits of rage and intimidation, and his inability to think logically about any situation that required him to apologize or acknowledge his mistakes. He withheld love, affection, money, and sex, while other times being a bit forceful in terms of each. He neglected our family and managed to isolate me and my children from those who loved us and saw through the situation.

As I sat at the library, I read story after story of people who were in emotionally abusive relationships. Their stories sounded eerily familiar. Their partner was involved in affair after affair. They had gone through countless efforts in therapy with their partner, with no relief. Trying to talk with the partner was one big circular, illogical conversation, that only left them feeling shameful, sad, scared, hopeless, and guilty.

It took me under two hours to read this book from cover to cover. I could not put it down, and I read it with chills down my spine the entire time. I knew I was not alone. By the time I finished the book, there were enough stories presented, and enough clinical evidence, that I finally realized that I, too, was being abused. All these years, believing there was something wrong with me, believing if only I changed him, he would finally love me enough to stay honest and faithful. All the time family, friends, even my kids, tried to warn me, yet I ignored their advice. I also could not ignore the fact that he had also made threats against me physically.

I sat at the table at the library, with tears rolling down my face. I thought back to the last few weeks with him. They hit an all-time high in terms of arguments, and the things he slung at me were awful. I finally acknowledged that I was truly afraid for myself, and for my children. Leading up to this point, I knew he was sick, but I thought I could help him. I believed that, when I said "I do" I was making a vow that meant I had to stick by him and help him through this. I thought that his cross was mine to bear, by the simple fact that he was my husband.

If the healing process taught me nothing else, it taught me that you can only heal yourself. There was no way possible that I could ever have convinced my husband that he was sick, or that there needed to be real change made in his actions. Every time I tried, the fight got louder and louder. He was telling me he didn't want to hear it, and very clearly, trying to convince me that it was all my fault, that I was the one with the problem.

He actually was right, partially. I was contributing to the problem. I had become so obsessed with holding onto a vision for my life where I believed I needed someone else to take care of me, that I was willing to force it, refusing to see him for the person he truly was. In holding onto this idea, I became so focused on trying to change him that it almost cost me my health, my career, and my relationship with my kids.

The only thing that I could change was myself.

I knew that night that I had a choice to make. I could either: continue down the road I had been on, feeling stuck in this situation and completely powerless, or I could stand up for myself and for my children, and decide that I was not going to allow this treatment any longer. I knew I did not want to stay stuck where I was. I knew that if I had any shot at making my dreams come alive, that I would have to fight for myself. Nobody was coming to save me, or my kids. I had to save myself, and in doing so, I could protect my children.

I started making some phone calls the next day, questioning everything he ever told me That night, I kicked him out, and went and filed a police report. The following morning, I filed for protection from abuse, which was, thankfully, granted. That afternoon, I also tried to have him involuntarily committed. Sitting in the room with the delegate and crisis worker, I was told, "Mrs. Miles, you have enough evidence to show this man needs serious help, but there is nothing we can do to help you. Based on the way the law is currently written, we cannot grant your petition. Thank you for your time." And as I was walking out of the hospital, the crisis worker came up to me and said, "I am so glad that you have the protection order in place. You did a good thing there. Turn around, keep your head in front of you, and never ever walk back into his path again."

I was stunned. I was angry. I was scared and confused. I felt defeated. I was able to get him away from me and my children but could not get him off the street. I knew the fight was just beginning, but now the kids and I could get some breathing room, if only for a few days. The following week, I had to face him in court. I was nervous, nauseous, and, literally, shaking in my boots. Standing before the judge, under oath, and in front of an entire courtroom filled with people, I had to have this final showdown with him.

For a moment, I almost had the order thrown out, believing that, if I could just get him to listen to me, he'd change, and things would be better. Then I remembered all of the times I asked him to get help, and he chose not to. I remembered the lies and manipulation. I remembered all of the horrible things he said to me, and about me, and the ways in which he threatened my safety. I thought about our kids, and about all of the ways he had hurt them, too. I wanted someone else to make this decision for me, or to tell me I was doing the right thing. Ultimately, I had to accept responsibility and choose for myself. This is where my vision for my life had to be so compelling that it pushed me through this nightmare. I had to hold tight to the vision I was pushing towards.

Accepting and honoring the vision is only half the battle. We must continue to live in alignment with that vision each and every day. This means showing up as the person we need to be in order to make that vision a reality. I came to realize that, as long as I allowed him to have power over me, my thoughts, my beliefs, and my actions and reactions, that vision would stay a vision. I had to choose to fully and completely acknowledge my personal power to create a life of happiness and peace. Part of taking back this power, ultimately, meant I had to forgive him. The moment I realized this; I could feel my entire body cringe. For a minute, I got angry, and thought "if I forgive him, he gets away with all the pain he caused."

Then, I accepted the fact that what was done was done. Nothing could change the past. I had to accept that forward progress could not happen while I was holding onto the anger. If I was truly going to let him go, I had to forgive him. I also knew that, if I was going to help others in the way that I truly wanted, I had to forgive. Holding onto the anger, pain, and frustration was only holding me back.

This was painful. I had to come to the realization and full acceptance, that his actions truly had nothing to do with me. It was never because of anything I did or said. It had nothing to do with a lack of my own worthiness for love. His actions were a direct result of who he is and how he sees and perceives his own reality. His life is based on his choices for who he believes he is, what he believes he deserves, and how he chooses to conduct himself based on his own experiences. It doesn't make it okay. There is no excuse for anyone to treat another person with such a lack of respect and with such hatred.

This meant that I had to also let go of the stories in my head that I had been telling myself for so long, accepting that there had to be at least some good in me after all.

I also had to acknowledge that, for the entire course of our relationship, I was one hundred percent responsible for my own actions and reactions. While he was choosing to act in a particular fashion, I, too, was choosing my own reality, based on my past experiences, my beliefs about who I was, and how I was supposed to show up as a wife and mother, and based on what I believed I deserved from life. I always had the power to choose. The choices I made were not in alignment with who I wanted to be, but I chose them anyway. I knew that I could not fully forgive him without also holding myself accountable and being able to find forgiveness for myself.

Acknowledging these truths, the fact that his behavior had nothing to do with me, and everything to do with him, and that I was responsible for my own actions, was a powerful moment. I could have compassion for his journey, while forgiving his actions, while simultaneously setting my soul free.

Then, I could choose again.

No matter the situation, you always have the power to choose again. Forgiveness and compassion forced me to look at him from a new point of view, one that no longer made me a victim and him the enemy. I held myself accountable for my actions and contributions to the situation, recognizing it as a chance to understand myself. It was not who I wanted to be. It never was. Now, I could see it, with crystal clearness, and then choose who I wanted to be from that moment forward. I could now move forward and take action on my life.

With that, I also gave him back his power to choose. Letting go of control was difficult for me. But ultimately, I had to realize that, if I wanted to keep my power of choice, I had to allow others to have theirs. Not easy, when there is the potential for rejection from someone you care about.

Forgiveness is the gift you give to your heart. It's the gift you give to your vision for your life. When you forgive, you release the pain of a situation from your heart. There's peace. There's clarity. You can move forward with ease. Forgiveness is about you.

As a side note, I cannot ignore this piece of synchronicity from the Universe...

It's ironic that, as I write this, we celebrate the Full Moon in Aries. Six months ago, the New Moon in Aries marked a time for transformation—the start of the process of transforming our lives to become a better version of ourselves, taking on projects and relationships and situations that foster our growth. With this came the awareness that we do not need to carry burdens that are actually, in fact, not our own. April was the time when I found myself standing at a campsite hearing that undeniable voice that said, "this is where you pivot." I had no idea what it meant, or the journey that was to unfold before me. All I knew was that the voice was loud, and it was a call that I could not deny.

For the next six months, I kept pivoting. Making new choices. Realizing that I alone need to stand up and make the decisions that reflect the person I wanted to be, and the life that I wanted to live. With each new obstacle, the outcome relied solely on my decisions. Nobody was coming to save me. I could sit there and wallow in fear, anger, worry, or frustration, or I could choose. Make a decision. Move.

I wrote my book. I thought that was what the pivot was supposed to be about. To my happy surprise, it was about so much more. Yes, I wrote the book. That gave me pause to sit back and reflect on my life and understand why situations and people came into my life. It made me stop and think about my responses to situations. I examined my mindset. It brought up a lot of emotions that I didn't realize were still lingering in the darkness. It was uncomfortable. It was messy. It was hard. I had to bring it all up in order to let it all go. Once I did that, once I let go of that darkness, I could remember how I wanted life to feel.

I found release.

Closing my bakery was closing a chapter in my life. I realized that the persona of the baker was not one that I chose for myself. Someone else told me "hey, you are a great baker, you should open a store." Based on that statement alone, which I had heard numerous times as a kid, I crafted a vision for something that I realized I never actually wanted. I enjoyed it, yes. But I didn't take the time to consider how I would run the business, and what I wanted to bring to the world with it. I didn't question it. I just accepted it as true for me, then, when the time was right, I dove head first into running a business I knew nothing about. I then resisted the process of manifesting the business that I was imagining. I wasn't vibrating with the essence of what or who I truly am.

I found closure.

Looking back, in those six months, my vision for my life became much stronger. I gained more confidence and respect for myself as a person, as a wife, as a mother, and as a business owner. I started to recognize my worth. While this process was not yet complete, the stronger the awareness, the more that did not align fell off the radar. This included people, places, situations, things. And the closing act—finally seeing the lies, deceit, manipulation, and abuse from my husband. Hearing his threats for what they were—threats—and making the decision to do something about it, instead of sitting back and living in fear, living in denial, and allowing my children to do the same. He was evicted because I filed for protection from abuse. We have not spoken since, except for a few text messages or sitting in a courtroom. And I knew that life would need to be very different, that I would need to be different.

I found strength.

It seems fitting now, with the Full Moon in Aries upon us, that this is a time for completion. I am much more self-aware. I get to choose my mood. I get to choose my actions, I get to choose my reactions, situations, expectations, thoughts, beliefs, emotions. I get to choose the people in my life. I set the boundaries and rules for how others interact, or not, with me. Understanding this gave me such a feeling of immense power over my life.

There is always an opportunity for change. For growth. For peace. We are called to recognize that opportunity, then decide whether we are going to seize it or not.

It's time to seize the moment. It's time to listen to your intuition. It's time to leave the past behind and start over. The best is yet to come. I had a vision for my life, and a mountain of fear and self-judgement standing between me and that vision. That's the way it goes. We know what is on the other side. Well, we hope we know what is on the other side, but realistically, all we can do is plan things out as best as possible, think it through, and then take action. Even then, there's no guarantee the plan will work the way we intended.

Sometimes, because we don't know, instead of taking action, we create excuses. We come up with a million reasons why now isn't the right time, or why we don't have enough education, or why we simply can't be the one to change the world. We feel the discomfort of change, and in the uncertainty of what life looks like down the path, so we stall ourselves. Suddenly, that huge, beautiful vision we created seems way out of our reach, and we feel small and insignificant and stuck in our own life.

You, my friend, are not small. Stop playing that way. While it might seem true, that's your mind playing tricks on you. Don't play into it. Your life matters! Your vision, and what you want to create in the world, matters. If you need to highlight that, post a reminder on your cell phone, send yourself a reminder text every day, do it! Do whatever it takes for you to remind yourself, constantly, until it's ingrained into your soul, that you are worthy of whatever you want. You just need to feel it, believe it, and then get to work.

So here, before we end this section, I want you to take some time and create a vision for your life. What do you want? Don't answer that in terms of what you think you should say, or what you think someone else will want you to say. Answer it in terms of what is, truly, in your heart. Because that is the only answer that matters. When you allow yourself the time and space to dream, and really hone in on the vision of the life you want, it makes the healing process a little less daunting. There becomes a purpose for the pain. You can see your "why". You know what you are working towards.

When you love yourself enough, daydreaming on a regular basis becomes an amazing tool. Give yourself time every day and consider what you want. What are you thinking? What actions do you do regularly? How do you show up in your life? And probably most important - how does it all feel? The day-to-day activities matter, for sure, but what do you want to feel, energetically, each and every day?

These are important questions to answer if you want to start to create change. And, they help with the healing process. Once you create your vision, you can start to craft affirmation statements that align with that vision. For example, my vision (or purpose) statement looked something like this...

I, Elizabeth Miles, am an author, life coach and speaker. I travel the world, teaching others that it is okay to take control of their lives, to stand in their power, and show up every day feeling peaceful, happy and fulfilled. I am passionate, creative, loving. I show up every single day for myself, my family, my clients, and my readers, listening, supporting them, and encouraging them to keep going, reminding them that their journey is worth it. I am confident in who I am. I live a life of peace and joy. I know who I am. I know what I am capable of. I know that I am safe and secure, and I know that I am worthy."

I will also add, that having a timeframe built in is helpful. It solidifies your vision. It's no longer "just a daydream", it's a plan, even if the details haven't all been worked out yet.

Having the compelling vision makes it easier to move through healing. You know what you are working for, and why. It prepares you to feel what you will feel when you are able to release the things that are not in your best interest to hold onto.

Once you have a vision statement, you can create goals that are centered around that vision. These can be daily, weekly, monthly, yearly. Setting the timeline further solidifies that, no matter what, you are going to accomplish this. By the time you get to this step, once you set some goals, you are gaining more and more momentum. You are starting to take action. It becomes a snowball effect. You put one foot in front of the other, slowly at first.

Eventually, this process becomes easier, so you start to move a little faster. You are seeing traction. Guess what? You are achieving your goals! Celebrate. You did it!

All because you took the time to love yourself enough to be honest with yourself about what you want in life.

Love yourself!

(Additional Letters from My Soul to Yours)

A LETTER FROM MY SOUL TO YOURS
(Talking to Your Higher Self),

In my dreams, I see you standing there, off in the distance. I hear you call my name, but you look off into the other direction. You are so close, yet so far away. Can you feel me standing there behind you? Do you hear me echo back to you?

I sit here under a blanket full of stars on this crisp, fall night, and my heart cries out to you. From across the silence, across the depths of loneliness, here I sit, waiting. I cannot see you. I cannot touch you. Yet I know the sound of your voice. I can feel your essence around me. Where are you? Will that first catch of our eyes click us into harmony in the physical realm, just as our souls beat together in the heavens?

I wonder—how can I miss that which I do not know? Except, I do know. I know you. We have always been together. Two perfect puzzle pieces, fitting together so snug and tight. Seamless. From here until eternity.

Love,
Yourself

DEAREST YOU,

You could not have known. You could not have seen. You were not supposed to before this very moment.

You had to go through it all. You had to learn the lessons. You had to get through the fire. A phoenix does not rise until its time. A butterfly cannot emerge from the cocoon before it is ready.

We all must endure our winter before spring can come.

You are strong! Look at what you have come through. Look back, just for a second, but never go back. Don't turn around only to head back into the fire.

You are on the other side. You made it. You survived.

Love,
Yourself

DEAREST ME,

I always stayed. I didn't fight the fear or turn and run from it. I lived in it, paralyzed to take any steps to help myself. I thought fear was a part of life, the way things were supposed to be. I was afraid to make friends, afraid to be myself, afraid to take risks, afraid to set boundaries and stand up for myself.

Over and over, I gave my power over to someone or something else entirely—all because I was afraid.

As a wife—I was too afraid to stand up for the boundaries I tried to set. I didn't leave when I was disrespected; I was too afraid. The situation kept getting worse. I then tried to control it even more, turning the relationship, my family, my entire life, into a constant battleground, with me playing detective all the time instead of acting as the loving wife.

So much time and energy gone. Wasted. And all for what? To find myself alone. To find myself sad, scared, and feeling broken. Not knowing who I am in this world, or what to do next.

No more! Today, I choose again! I choose me!

Love,
Yourself

DEAR YOU,

Shine your light.
   Be the light.
   You are an angel—use your wings and fly.
   It's time for you to soar.
   Before you can soar, you have to cut the anchors that are weighing you down.

   Love,
      Yourself

CHAPTER 6

Boundaries

DEAR SELF,

Stop trying to prove your worth. Do you know how valuable you are?

Love,
    Yourself

DEAR SELF,

Why am I always left holding the bag? I am always left picking up the pieces from everyone else's stuff. I take care of the kids, the house, the bills. I manage the schedules, the rides, the doctor's appointments. I listen to everyone's drama, and I worry that they are going to be okay. Meanwhile, who's worrying about me? My life is on hold. Nobody is checking in on me. Nobody is supporting me. Nobody encourages me or asks if I need anything.

I feel so alone. Why do I keep giving so much to everyone? It takes away so much from myself.

Love,
Yourself

OH! BOUNDARIES. WHAT EXACTLY ARE THEY? I have heard that phrase "uphold your boundaries" for a while now. While I thought I understood, I really only recently truly "got" it.

Boundaries, in their simplest, come down to these questions:

- Are you showing yourself the respect that you deserve?
- How confident do you feel?
- Do you say what you mean, and do what you say?
- Are you using your power, or giving it away to other people or things?
- And, my favorite: Do you trust that little voice in your head that offers you guidance and direction, even when that voice makes absolutely zero sense at all?

Like the boundaries of a property, set to delineate where one piece of land ownership ends and another begins, the same is true for personal boundaries. When you are in a relationship, you set your own boundaries to delineate yourself from the other person. To accept and tolerate only that which you want for your life.

Setting personal boundaries is an act of self-love. In setting these boundaries, we decide how we treat ourselves, and how others will treat us as well. In all actuality, if everyone was walking around setting and upholding their own boundaries, and respecting the boundaries of others, there would never be an imbalance of power in any relationship. Ultimately, it's a choice we make, usually so that we gain what is perceived as love and desire from another person. There is danger in not upholding our own boundaries. We leave ourselves open and vulnerable, potentially exposed to control and manipulation.

Setting and maintaining strong boundaries means that you are saying "no" to the things that you do not want, and "yes" only to what truly matters to you. It means that you are standing up for yourself, taking an assertive (not aggressive) role in your own life, and, most importantly, not getting taken advantage of. With strong boundaries, you do what you say and say what you mean, respecting your own wishes enough to uphold and honor them. In this way, you become a leader in your own life, taking personal responsibility for what you do, what you say, and how you feel. You are using your power to create the life that truly aligns with the person you want to be. In doing so, you are also acknowledging and respecting the boundaries of others, giving them the power to show up as the person they truly are.

Whether they recognize and accept their personal power or not is a choice that they make for themselves. Whether they choose to respect your boundaries is a choice that they make for themselves. Part of you taking your power back involves choosing how you respond, or don't.

Let me ask you a few questions.

Do you say "yes" when you really mean and want to say "no?" If this happens, do you get this knot of regret in your stomach? Is there a particular person this happens most often with? What is the result of saying "yes?" How does it impact you? If you could wave a magic wand, what would you like to say, truthfully?

As an example, as parents, our kids ask us all the time for rides to their friends' houses, or rides to work, or rides to the mall (I know mine do). We feel obligated to say "yes" because, well, they are our children, and we need to provide for them. We want to be there. But what if they consistently ask you at the very last minute for a ride, and you are in the middle of a big project that is important to you? How does that make you feel?

For me, I found myself saying "yes" because I didn't want a fight. I didn't want to seem like a bad mom. But I would answer with an eye roll, a sigh, and an "okay" of frustration. I felt taken advantage of, that the work I was doing wasn't as important.

That did not feel good at all.

As an alternative, we were able to come up with a system that allowed me to set and uphold a boundary, and my kids would get where they wanted to go. This can work in any number of ways, but for us, I encouraged my kids to try to set plans a day in advance, or more when possible, with as much detail as possible. That meant working out rides, money, times, etc., so that I could work out my schedule in a way that made sense. We also set a time each week to sit down and go over the upcoming agenda for the week, so that they knew when I had plans to work, and I knew when they had plans to be somewhere. This way, we were all on the same page. They knew my work was important to me. I knew their plans were important to them. We were able to work out a system so that I didn't feel like I had to stop mid-paragraph if I was writing in order to carpool kids to the mall. And it gave them a sense of power and responsibility for their own actions and choices, helping them to think ahead, plan, and communicate.

There needs to be clear consequences when the boundaries are crossed. In the example above, if my kids asked me last minute for a ride, I would ask them if there was any other possibility to get there, assuming I was in the middle of something. Could another parent possibly take them, and I could pick up? Was Uber an option (when it was age appropriate)? If there were no other options, I had the choice to say "yes" or "no." They understood that a "no" meant that I was in the middle of working, and that was important to me so that I could maintain our household expenses. This became even more important when I became a single parent. There was nobody else to rely on to ask for rides. There was one of me and multiple of them. They knew that there was the possibility of a "no." Because we were able to discuss that ahead of time, they were very understanding and receptive. This made it easier to say "no" and not feel bad about it.

Let me be clear. This is not easy to recognize, and it's not easy to stop doing either. Despite our best intentions, we, unfortunately, can't just wake up and say, "I will no longer be controlled." Usually! I say that, because eventually (hopefully) you will find a reason to do so. Your "why" becomes greater than the situation you are currently in, and then, you are on your way. It takes practice.

To set boundaries, it's important to first understand your worth. Otherwise, the boundaries get set, but then we allow others to step over the boundary and take away our power. We get taken advantage of. This would happen to me any time someone would: ask me to meet for coffee but show up twenty minutes late. Anytime someone lied to me. Anytime someone said "I am sorry" only to then go back to doing that same thing over again. Anytime someone failed to show me simple respect.

Recognize, too, that it's possible for you to ignore your own boundaries. Every time you allow someone else to disrespect you, and you shake it off without dealing with it even though you know you should, or you know it makes you upset, you are ignoring your boundaries. The goal: stand up for the respect you deserve from other people—and require that same level of respect from yourself.

Ask yourself: whose "yes" are you playing out in your life? Who is it that you don't want to disappoint? Who do you feel you need or want approval from? And, most importantly, why?

Know what you stand for, what you don't, and be willing to honor both.

Communication is key here. Set clear intentions and expectations with the people around you. Keep in mind— strengthening boundaries takes practice. Recognize, too, that it takes practice for the person on the other end to accept this from you. They might not like it at first, or ever. That's okay. Keep practicing setting and upholding those boundaries. Those that respect you will accept and honor them. Those who don't will likely fall away from your life. While the intention is not to lose people, it happens. This is an okay thing. When those people fall away, there is room for people who love, respect, and support you to come into your life, making it easier for you to have strong boundaries. It takes much less energy to maintain these boundaries because you don't have to fight through the resistance of those who refuse to accept them.

And guess what? When this happens, it becomes easier for you to move forward on the things that make you happy. You spend less time feeling angry or upset or frustrated, or fighting to stand up for yourself. You have more energy to feel good, with energy to create whatever it is you want.

To be fair—I did my share of overstepping boundaries as well. It goes both ways. Once you can see the importance of setting boundaries, though, you are then more likely to respect those of others.

Once you know your worth, you set a higher standard for your life. You know what you want. You know that you are capable of getting it, and worthy and deserving to keep it. There's power in that. For me, the revelation happened when I made this connection: ...

By setting and upholding boundaries, we confirm to the Universe all that we claimed we wanted is actually, in fact, true. Read that again.

We create the vision for our life. We know what we want. But if we spend our time allowing situations that don't align with the desire, we are telling the Universe, "yeah, that big dream I wanted, yeah, that's only sorta, kinda important to me." It's much more challenging to manifest from this perspective. Actually, it's impossible.

But...when you show up for yourself, uphold your boundaries, and act in alignment with the thing you want—that's when the magic happens. Because the Universe gets the sign "yup—that's what she really wants."

I will give you an example...

Once my marriage ended, eventually I felt ready to welcome someone new into my life. Scary, really, because it had been such a long time. After I gave myself some time to heal, I started thinking about the type of romantic love I wanted to call into my life. I gave myself some time and permission to dream. The first few guys I talked with were nice, sure, but none of them treated me with respect or decency. It felt comfortable and familiar for a few days...then I realized, "hey, wait a minute.... this is what I had and left...no way am I going back to that. Thanks, but no thanks. I am waiting on something and someone who appreciates what I bring to the table." That simple act of acknowledging what I did not want, and then letting it go, was telling the Universe that the new dream for romance is the one that I truly want in my life. By letting go of the old stories, we can manifest the new dreams into reality.

Love yourself!

CHAPTER 7

Intuition

DEAR SELF,

Is the pain of staying where you are now greater than your fear of the unknown?

Love,
    Yourself

DEAR SELF,

You are a work of art, truly magical. And you shine! See it! Feel it! Believe it! Then share that magic with the world. There is a spark inside of you, a light that needs to be shared. Do you know what it is? Are you able to express it? Isn't it time you found out?

Love,
Yourself

HAVE YOU HEARD THE EXPRESSIONS "trust your gut" or "follow your heart?"

These phrases are encouraging us to trust ourselves. We all have intuition, which is an inner knowing, a sense of what is right or wrong for our highest good. When you are loving yourself, following your intuition comes naturally. You set clear boundaries, and uphold them, and you are comfortable and confident in who you are. With that strong sense of self, it's easy to know when your intuition is telling you to "go for it" or "back off." When you love yourself, it becomes easy to trust your gut in service of your heart.

For each of us, the voice manifests a little differently. Maybe it's ringing in your ears, or a knot in your stomach or your heart. Maybe you hear a little voice telling you your next move. Maybe you just have this sense of knowing, almost like you can see what's coming next. Your intuition tells you "that's not really a good idea" or "make a right turn instead of going left" or "wear the purple shirt today instead of the red."

Most importantly, your intuition is going to tell you "go for your dreams, and here's the next step to make it happen." No matter how it shows itself, when your intuition is fired up, it's going to show you the right steps to take, and those options will feel light and airy to you.

At the other end of the spectrum, we have your ego. Your ego is the voice that tells you "you can't" or "you shouldn't" or says, "you are crazy; that's impossible." In terms of healing and changing your life, when your ego is doing the talking, the options it presents will often feel heavy. The route the ego wants you to take is, literally, weighing you down and holding you back from moving forward.

In essence, intuition and fear are trying to achieve the same outcome. Both are there to keep us safe, and both are there to help us acknowledge our desires. And desire can be a good thing—that's how we set goals. We desire to achieve something different for ourselves. There is nothing wrong with that. The difference, though, is that intuition is based on love, while ego is fear-based. That's why, when you are loving yourself, it's easier to hear intuition. When the ego is fired up, you know what you want, but will make every excuse in the book as to why it won't happen. You are afraid of failure. Afraid you will be laughed at. Afraid that you are going to die trying. Ego wants you to stay where you are, cozy and tucked into your current state of affairs, where you have everything (it seems) under control. Your intuition wants to push you, make you grow, so that you can achieve your goals, and it's cheering you on all along the way. Intuition tells you, "this is going to be uncomfortable…do it anyway."

When you are not in a state of loving yourself, it's easier to sit back and believe that you can't. It's easier allow resistance to stop you from doing what you know you should. It's easier to sit back and let life pass you by because your ego is telling you to stay put.

Your ego is a liar. Fear is a liar.

Have you ever been lied to by a friend, and you knew what they were saying was a lie? Have you ever gotten this strong, undeniable hunch to do or say something that seemed out of the blue? To go right when you would normally go left?

How does that feel? How does that hunch come to you? Remember that, because it is critically important that you know what your intuition sounds and feels like. That way, the next time you hear that voice inside of you saying, "you are crazy; don't do it," you will know if it is your ego, or your intuition.

Your ego is lying.

When we are first starting out, just beginning to go through our healing process, your intuition might sound very quiet. And you might not be sure if you can trust it. It's like a muscle. The more you use it, the stronger it becomes. So the next time your intuition tells you to act, do whatever it is telling you to do, just move. Once you

90

do, it gets a little louder next time. If you doubt what that voice is saying, question it. In the beginning, your ego might try to sabotage your intuition, and since you don't have strong boundaries yet, and don't really trust yourself, it might be hard to tell the difference. Ask yourself the question again. Ask it a third time if you have to. Eventually you will start to know when your ego is trying to stop you and when your intuition is trying to warn you.

I will give you an example...

A few years ago, I was on my way to meet a client. As I got into my car, I planned to put on a particular playlist. But my intuition was telling me to play something else entirely, and it didn't make much sense. I ignored it at first, but the voice came back a second time, then a third. Finally, I listened. When I put on the song my intuition was telling me to listen to, I realized that my heart was trying to send me a message about something I needed to heal from.

The next time you have this seemingly crazy urge to play a particular song, or you wake up with it in your head, think "what is my intuition trying to tell me here."

Also, recognize that when thoughts repeat, it's usually intuition. Your heart is seeking to connect with you so that you can take action and grow. It's always there, ready to remind you of your next right action. We resist it. We don't want to listen. If we listen, that means we are going to have to move out of our comfy state of affairs. We know it's going to take action to achieve what we want. We'd rather sit back and let the world pass by or let ourselves believe that we need someone else to do the work for us, or that we need someone else's approval in order to move ahead.

Sometimes, my intuition tells me to stop and rest. I get subtle cues in my body at first, maybe a little sleepy. I don't always listen, particularly when I put myself on a deadline, or make a list that I want to complete. Staying so rigid in my planning is one of the ways

I stop myself from listening to my intuition. I get so stuck in the details and the plan.

Except that, when I don't listen, those cues get louder. Eventually, I end up exhausted to the point where I have to stop. Those are moments when my intuition is screaming to me "hey...you need to take a minute, there's something you are missing."

And it's not that I don't like the rest. It's more that I am afraid of what will happen if I take it. We are programmed to believe that busy equals productive and productive equals success. For me, that doesn't work. That actually prevents my creativity from flowing through. I can't do my best work, in anything, when I am in that state.

So how do we trust that our intuition actually put us on a better path? Begin with the lesson you learned from the experience. What did it teach you? How can that information change you now? And to where would the other option have led you?

When I was moving through my divorce, particularly at the very early stages, I was very tempted to get myself back out in the dating world pretty quickly. Let's face it, being alone can suck sometimes. Through that, though, I had to force myself to slow down the pace and give myself time to reflect on what had just happened, and what went wrong in the previous relationship. My intuition regularly popped up to slow me down. I would get tired. Sick. Or I would start to notice myself feeling "off."

When I made myself take a minute, I could sit back and listen. In those moments, I could see that I was ignoring important warning signs in terms of what someone was saying, or how they were acting. I remembered that I was not the same person that I was when I got married. I had all of this experience and self-awareness. I had to use this time to remember who I was, *in this moment*, otherwise, I ran the risk of running right back into the situation I just left.

I just got a hard lesson on boundaries, what they were, how to uphold them, and why they were important. I came to realize that, just because I now knew what a boundary was, maintaining those boundaries did not happen automatically. This was a severely under-developed muscle that needed to be worked out, quite a bit, in order to be strong enough to keep me from making the same relationship mistakes.

I did not want to feel alone either. One night, it hit me; all those years, I pushed so hard to control the one thing I was most afraid of—being alone. In all reality, that was the situation I ended up creating. I was alone. And it turned out to be the best thing that could ever happen to me.

Are you tilting your head and wondering, "what the heck is she talking about?"

Because I was so afraid of being alone, I was willing to do anything necessary to force the relationship to work. Be more controlling. Try harder to show more love. The one who handled the bills, carpools, the grocery shopping. I was the one who dealt with the house cleaning, planned the date nights. The list could go on. The important part is—because I was so afraid, I gave up my ability to be uniquely and fully myself. I was happy to do those things, don't get me wrong, but I did them out of fear, and I never truly felt safe enough to stand up for what I knew in my heart was a better scenario—that we were partners and needed to be working together to make things work. I negotiated away that power. I had zero boundaries, and I completely ignored my intuition. In doing so, I also stopped being happy. I isolated myself from the world, making myself fully available when my husband needed me to be. I thought I was doing the right thing, being the dutiful wife. The longer that went on, though, the harder it became for me to remember that I had goals and dreams, and that I was smart, and driven to make a difference.

After you release the situations that have hurt you, you might feel a little bit broken. Acknowledge this. But also know that it's time to put yourself back together, and you get to decide which pieces you want to keep from the old version of yourself, and which you no longer need. You get to decide how you want the pieces to fit. What do you want the new you to look like when the process is complete?

For me, I knew where I wanted my life to go. I had to figure out the best way to get my life on that path. The best way for me to do that was to start by remembering what I loved and enjoyed in life. Shortly after my husband left, someone asked me to describe myself. Other than "recently separated" and "mom," I could not find any other words to describe who I was. My identity was lost completely. That was uncomfortable, particularly because I didn't want to live and define myself by my situation.

How do you get reacquainted with yourself?

Allow yourself time and space to create and play. Go on an adventure to understand, define, and refine who you are.

All too often, we get caught up in what other people will think of our sparkle, our magic, and we then use that as reason to hide. Our light seems to dim…

But it is always there, shining bright. It's who we truly are, and who we are meant to be in the world. Sometimes, we forget. Sometimes, we lose our voice. That does not change the essence of what's deep within our soul. Who we are at the core of our being cannot change. The only thing that changes is our ability to see and know it, and then show up in that capacity in the world.

And when we do—woah baby!—sparks fly, and then the magic really unfolds. Synchronicity begins to happen. People, places, situations are put in place that attract more of what you truly desire for your life. You deserve that! The only question becomes...

Will you CHOOSE it?

It really comes down to making a choice. Most of the time we tend to forget how powerful we really are, and that there is always the opportunity to choose. We can choose to stay where we are, choose to be unhappy and unfulfilled, choose to not live our purpose.

In some ways, that seems like the easy thing to do. It doesn't require effort.

Or does it?

I believe it requires the effort to prove that we are not capable, or worthy, of success, or greatness. We go to great lengths to prove this right. I know I did. There are things that come up in life; situations, feelings, expectations that we just refuse to see. In reality, they are not hidden at all. We don't want to believe it could be true.

Look how long I stayed in my marriage! Almost twenty years! I could not allow myself to see what was really happening right before my eyes. If I had, I would have had to make the effort to take action to change the situation, which meant doing the uncomfortable thing—leaving! Being a single parent! Maybe working two jobs so I could get my career off the ground. It would mean I would have to ask myself some very tough, hard, difficult questions, that would leave me feeling very uncomfortable.

And, let's face it...who wants that?

The alternative, though, is we make those tough choices, and ask the difficult questions. I realized that, by being honest, and I mean brutally honest, with myself, I allowed myself to weigh the options in a new way. I asked myself things like "how do I want to feel? And "what do I really want my life to look like?" What is the worst that could happen if I decide to change this?"

It's scary, because you don't really know where the questions will take you. For me, I began to understand that I wanted so much more out of life. And the more I worked on myself, allowed myself to heal, and allowed my voice to be heard, the more I was, in fact, proving to myself that I actually could do the things I really didn't want to do. And when I realized that and began to make the connection with how I wanted to feel, and with my true, authentic voice, there was no alternative but to pivot. I knew what had to be done. In hindsight, I knew it all along. But I got to the point in my life where I couldn't sit back and not take action. That blindness was not serving me, or my kids, or my clients, or my purpose.

If you are truly listening to yourself, to your intuition, you will be able to see the right path for you. When things are not going well, anxiety flares up. You no longer feel light and happy. You might get tired. Those are all signs of a block in energy. It's happening from somewhere, or something, or someone. It's important to listen and trust that what you feel is real, and true. Then follow the path that it takes you down. You will get where you want to be.

This is not easy. I know. If it were, everyone would do it, and everyone would be living in a state of total and absolute bliss.

Our intuition is never wrong. Ever. If it takes you down the wrong path, it wasn't your intuition, it was your ego. Your intuition feels like, fun. The ego feels heavy, resistant. You can usually feel it in the pit of your stomach. When you put a question out into the Universe, you will get an answer. Sometimes, it's something we don't want to hear, so our ego kicks in so we feel better. We need to question that every chance we get. When you have a thought that you believe is your intuition, ask the question again, and a third time if you have to. And then tune into yourself. Tune into your body. Does the answer feel right? Be honest with yourself about this. Are you trying to force something into the world, or avoiding the truth about something?

For me, I had to get out there and try new things. I found classes, took myself on road trips, grabbed a journal and wrote in the park, found new coffee houses. I took the time to explore. It felt clunky and unnatural at first, but this shook me out of my comfort zone enough pretty fast, and I remembered that, before all the chaos started, I was a pretty fun person to be around. I remembered that I enjoyed new experiences, new people, and living life. That was key to getting me back on the path I knew I belonged on.

I realized that being alone was a gift. In those times when I was alone, I was able to rediscover old parts of my spirit that went missing somewhere in the last twenty years, as well as discover new pieces that I hadn't been able to find until that point. There was peace there. One Sunday morning, I woke up to the sound of peace and quiet in the house. Instead of rushing out of bed, worrying about taking the dog for a walk, or who was going to make breakfast, I just sat there. I meditated. I sat and enjoyed the coziness of my blanket and pillow. I read a book from cover to cover.

I realized that I liked it! That this was my new normal, and it was not such a bad place to be. Because, in this space, I was able to be fully present in the moment. There was no fear. There was no anxiety about what my husband was doing, or who he was talking to. There was no fear of another fight when he got home. There was no fear at all. Just me, being present, in the moment, accepting myself and this time I was gifted, to remember that I am truly okay just as I am.

I also started to really see how our energy radiates out into the world around us. A few months after my divorce was final, I ran into one of my daughter's past teachers. What she said to me shook me to my core...

"Oh my goodness! It is so great to see you. I almost didn't recognize you. Please don't take this the wrong way, but you finally look happy."

I felt my head tilt to the right a little. I felt myself stare at her and blink. I took a breath. I had no idea how to respond. She continued on to say...

"Every time I saw you back then, you never looked happy. There was no life coming out of you. You were there. I saw you. I heard you. But you weren't really alive. You are here today, though, and, girl, you are glowing! And it is so good to see you finally come to light."

Woah, baby!

At that point, she hadn't even heard what happened. Truthfully, she didn't need to know. The energy spoke for itself, all because I gave myself time to embrace the situation, embrace how I was feeling, get honest with what was working and what wasn't, let go, and rebuild.

The biggest takeaway—give yourself time.

Climbing a mountain takes work. When we come into the world, on a physical level we, unfortunately, do not get a choice what our mountain is. Maybe it's a bad relationship. Maybe it's abuse. Maybe it's issues with money or addiction. Our soul knows. Our soul chose this reality and agreed to come into this lifetime and have these experiences to give you the choice—stay stuck or grow. You can always pivot. You can always choose a new path for yourself. There is always the option of choosing a new path and trying again.

Truth bomb time!

Nobody else is responsible for achieving your goals. Nobody else is responsible for living your life. Nobody can live your truth for you.

Decide. What do you want? What makes your heart skip a beat? And do you feel worthy enough to call that into your life? Take a stand for yourself!

The truth is: healing can only really begin when we are ready to feel worthy enough to release that which is holding us back. If you are walking around convinced that you want to create change for your life, but are waiting for someone else to tell you to move, that there is a curse over your head so can never work out, that someone's out to get you, or going to do it for you, or needs to tell you what to do, then you are not in a state of feeling worthy. Unfortunately, we tend to sabotage ourselves when it comes to this area of life. Why would you bother to try to heal when you don't feel worthy of being healed? Why go after something you do not truly and inherently believe you deserve?

You won't. Well, you might try, but it tends to not be quite as long-lasting of an effort.

Loving yourself enough to show up and do the work that needs to be done to heal, to live your purpose, requires the understanding that, in fact, nobody is coming to save you. Nobody can do it for you. Sure, there are resources to help you along the way. This book, for example. Therapy. Coaching. Classes. Workshops. Energy healing. I could go on.

We start these things with the best of intentions. We want something else. But so often we forget to sit back and think about exactly what it is that we truly want, and we don't take time to connect what we want to feeling like we deserve it. We just know that we don't feel good, and want to feel better.

Here's one tiny secret, though…set the goal and then *fake it 'til you make it.*

Find whatever modality is going to work best for you and commit to it wholeheartedly, with the understanding that the real motivation comes from within you. You might not believe your worth entirely at first. Move anyway. What is it that is going to push you forward? Focus on that one thing, and don't lose sight of what you want to accomplish. The more action you take, the more you build credibility with yourself. Small actions over time will help you to see, feel, and believe just how worthy you are.

Understand that the plan might change along the way. That is okay. The more action you take, the more you start to understand what it is you want. You can refine the steps as you go. Just move.

And always, always, always, take full responsibility for your thoughts and actions. What you put out into the world matters, and it is your responsibility to make sure it aligns with who you want to be.

Have you ever said, "but he/she makes me so __ (insert emotion here)"_?

Guess what?

Nobody made you feel that way.

You chose to feel that way. And you can choose to feel something else entirely.

For years, I believed that those around me were doing things TO me. That my beliefs about myself were because of someone else's actions towards me. And my reactions turned into just that—reactions.

Once I realized I could choose something else entirely, that I could let go of their actions and focus elsewhere...woah—things started to change completely.

I had to first start with recognizing that I was worthy enough to make the change. Once I got into motion, I had to keep reminding myself that I was worthy enough to keep moving forward.

So, start there. Start with your self-worth. You are one person on a planet of billions of people. There is nobody else exactly like you. You are priceless. But it's not enough for me to tell you. You have to believe it. To feel it in your soul. At bare minimum choose to try!

Step two to healing becomes the belief that you can. The belief that you will truly make a change. That this time, it's for real. For good.

Step three becomes the willingness to do the work and step four becomes the determination to keep working towards your vision, even when things get hard, because they will. Our ego likes to mess with us. Let's face it, the healing process puts us in a pretty vulnerable state. It's totally heart driven. Our ego does not want us to stay so open, so the ego tends to pop in when our defenses are at their lowest, trying to regain some control and order over our mind.

You need to have the determination that you can and will overcome this. Trust yourself, that your intuition is strong, and will get you through.

Defining our vision and goals are important pieces of the healing puzzle. In my experience, though, in the beginning, we just want the pain to stop. We want to get out of that hopeless state, where you feel stuck. That's the rock bottom point where you make the pivot. From there, the other steps fall in line. Once you begin to feel a little more in control, it becomes a little easier to think about what you really want for your life. The muck of the problems and the chaos they bring, blur the visions. Start ridding yourself of the muck, and the vision gets much clearer.

Let the dust settle. Adjust to your new surroundings. You have just climbed a mountain. Rest. Breathe. Take some time to nourish your soul and ease into the healing process.

- Sleep.
- Sit in nature.
- Make yourself a pot of soup.
- Put your feet up and watch a movie.
- Whatever it is, be gentle and kind to yourself.

It's easy and natural to want to just keep going. First, if we are moving, it means we are busy, and if we are busy then we can't be thinking about the pain that we just experienced. That causes us to shove down the pain and bury it again without having to actually heal and move on. Plus, we are programmed with the "go, go, go" mentality. We are raised to believe that if we are not moving, we are just wasting time and space.

Neither of these are true!

So, if you find yourself thinking this, stop and challenge it. Where does that come from? How is it benefitting you?

If we are not moving, it means we have come to a resting spot. We are reflective, planning, and focusing. We are setting up for the next big climb. With this rest, we have new information, newfound knowledge to help make the next part of our journey a little bit easier. We need to assimilate to the newness, decide how our new tools will be used, and then plan the strategy for what comes next. We get to listen to our heart.

For me, I knew it was time to get moving when I looked around at my room and got so frustrated with the literal, physical mess I was sitting in. Up until that point, I was so distracted with the chaos, and felt so bad about myself, that I let quite a few things go. There was clutter piled everywhere. My kitchen was a mess. I looked around at my house and realized that how my house looked reflected exactly how I felt on the inside.

After I gave myself some time to take in what happened, I woke up one day and was ready to move. That first tiny step came with me cleaning my room. I felt a sense of pride and accomplishment that I wanted to go further and clean the next room. It wasn't perfect at first, but it was a start. Over time, I also began to notice my kids following suit. They were no longer living in the chaos, and started to expect more for themselves and their own immediate surroundings. When I noticed that, I also noticed that my relationship with each of them changed. We were all laughing again. I was so grateful.

Rest. Then, and only then, when you are ready, get moving. It does not have to take long, but long enough for you to be able to stand up, head high, feeling proud of all that you just accomplished and recognizing how strong you truly are.

You are never stuck. You are never lost. You are never alone.

Love yourself!

CHAPTER 8

Energy is Everything

DEAR SELF,

I am happy to say that I finally feel like myself again. I am not as tired and drained as I once was. My body doesn't hurt all the time. This is amazing, but why? What happened that I feel so much more alive again? How do I keep this trend moving in this positive direction? I know I can do it, and I am open to the discovery.

Love,
    Yourself

WE ARE MADE UP OF ENERGY. It's everywhere. Think of energy as your internal body language. There's a flow to the energy within you. Even if you don't believe in energy healing, or things like reiki, think about a time when you felt upset, angry. Where did you feel that in your body? What did it feel like? Can you describe it? That anger likely caused an energy block, even if it was only temporary. Another good example is the end of a relationship. What does heartbreak feel like? For me, there's a heaviness in the chest. It's tight, tense. That is the sign of a block in the energy flow in your body.

Have enough of those blocks come up, and not be released, and we tend to feel depleted, worn down, burn out. Our energy is moving towards keeping us in a fight or flight response, rather than a flow state.

We want to keep the energy flowing. It's a critical component to the healing process. You can start by raising your awareness for where you feel emotions, and how you feel them, in your body. The more in tune you become, you allow yourself to adjust as needed. To pivot.

Learn how to manage your energy. Are you spending your time juggling fifteen different balls in the air when you are really only crazy passionate about, maybe, five? When you put your energy in so many places, you dilute your capacity to be effective in any one area. Your reserves get low. In essence, you burn out.

Easier said than done, right?

I had no idea about energy until I started working with a coach. I thought she was going to help me stay on track with weight loss, until one day she said "hey, what's going on with your energy?" That opened a dialogue I never expected.

Within each one of us is a series of energy sites called chakras. The goal is to have the chakras opened, with energy flowing through us consistently all the time. In some cases, though, situations come up that block the flow of energy within us.

I remember looking at an image that my first energy coach drew. She identified energetic nodes along my solar plexus chakra, the center for establishing and upholding boundaries and confidence in our life (go figure). These nodes were blocking my ability to manifest much in my life, because I lacked the confidence to take necessary steps forward. I was negotiating bits and pieces of myself away, giving away my own power and personal freedom, in exchange for the perception of love and attention. This further impacted me, in that I was not confident enough to use my voice, stand up for myself when needed, or speak my thoughts and opinions into the world.

I needed to work on healing my root chakra as well. Lots of root work to be done! Think of a tree in the forest. It needs strong roots in order to stabilize itself in a forest filled with other trees. We are similar in that regard. We need to have strong roots grounding us into our physical body, into our existence, so that we feel safe and secure.

And the most amazing part of this new awareness—she was able to see and feel all of this, simply by tuning into my energy. I hadn't really told her much yet, but she saw my energy, as it appeared in that moment. She saw the blocks, brought them to my awareness, and then I could work towards removing them.

I started making connections. I felt so tired because I was giving my energy away to things that really didn't matter in the grand scheme of what I wanted to create. There were people asking me to do things I didn't really want to do, and I was too afraid to say no. I thought I had to control everything, so I was also inserting myself into tasks and projects unnecessarily. I believed that I was not strong enough, or good enough, to be seen how I wanted to be seen in my life, so I negotiated myself away.

Life can be a very busy endeavor for all of us. Inundated with tasks and to-do lists, we want to get more done with less time. We strive for efficiency, fitting as much as possible, as fast as possible, in the same twenty-four hours of the day that we had yesterday. We look for better ways to manage our time—apps, calendars, reminders on our cell phone, blocking out your schedule. There are lots of methods for budgeting our time to "fit it all in." And they are important, but it's even more important to manage our energy.

While we all have the same twenty-four hours in a day, we each have our own, unique energetic makeup. My energy needs and availability are different than yours. When we understand this, and then allow ourselves to understand our individual energetic requirements, it becomes easier to get into the flow of our own life. We can heal through what needs to be healed, at our own pace, accept what we can and cannot control, and grant ourselves a little bit of grace when the dishes don't get washed or put away because we were busy spending time with our kids, because it was more important for us to create those connection moments than it was to have clean silverware. How we use our energy is a choice.

When you use your energy in a means that works for you, you are more productive, because you focus only on the tasks that are most important. You are making the best use of your time in a given day. There's a tremendous amount of personal freedom in that. How much sleep we get each night, the people we spend our time with, what we think about during the day, how we feel are all things that impact the energy that we have available.

Maybe you have heard this question—what is it, that thing, that motivates you? What is it that sets your soul on fire; that you are so passionate about, you can't stop thinking about it?

That, my friends, is your purpose. Your purpose is the core of your being, who you truly are. When you are honest and truthful with yourself about your actions and intentions, and then allow yourself to act only in ways that are in alignment with your purpose, you feel more energized. It's easier to build new habits, because you are only focusing on the habits that resonate with the person you actually want to be, and it becomes easier to let go of the thoughts, beliefs, behaviors that are completely unrelated. We are so in tune with being us, with being happy, and with that feeling of freedom that comes when we are truly living an authentic life.

As an example, there are those who recommend blocking time each day or week, or at specific intervals, to write a book, mapping out the content so that they have a plan of attack for each writing session. This is an example of managing time, not managing energy. For me, if I try to write a book in this manner, I would still likely be on the first chapter of book number one. I would have a perpetual case of writer's block. Once I figured out how my energy worked, I was able to write with a lot more ease. When I have those creative sparks, I use my time to write. If I get a spark but am not in a place where I can sit down and start writing sentences, I use my phone to take notes, so that I don't lose my thoughts. Then, I can go back and add those notes to my manuscript. Likewise, when I sit down to create, I do so until the energy for that task is gone, not when the timer goes off saying I should stop. If I start to get tired, I stop. If I find myself losing focus, I stop. In these moments, I recognize that it's a challenge for me to create my best work, and I don't believe I can be of much use to you if I am not using my energy in the best way possible to bring my A-game.

As a side note: sometimes, your purpose becomes your career. This does not have to be the case. It is totally okay if your purpose is not your profession.

Energy is everything!

Try to take a step back from whatever situation you are facing right now. Ask yourself:

- What is going on?
- What do you think about it? And be truthful with yourself.
- How does it make you feel emotionally?

- When you are considering your feelings, try to get as descriptive as possible. It's one thing to say "this makes me angry" but there are many faces to anger. Are you seething? Hurt? Frustrated? Try to get as specific as possible.
- What is your body language saying as you think about it? Where do you feel it in your body?
- Are you clenching your teeth or fists? Are you holding your breath?
- Is there a knot in your stomach? Are you getting neck pain? Headaches?

Observe it. Don't judge it. Don't react. Just look at it from the outside.

Why should we care? Because once we understand how a situation makes us feel, we can start to identify it to how we feel in our body and then begin to connect that with how our energy is impacted. Your feelings are your feelings, neither right nor wrong, yet we allow them to take over sometimes, dominating our actions and thoughts. As an example, because we "feel" angry, we act out accordingly. The reaction is not always positive and not always in our best interest. Because we aren't monitoring our energy, it might be too late before we realize that our feelings have taken over. This makes it even more imperative that we observe our thoughts, from a neutral perspective, and understand how those thoughts feel for us.

It's also important to recognize that you might not always know what you are feeling, except to say that you aren't yourself, feel tired, or depressed. That's okay. Take note of that, too. The more you practice understanding your energy, and your thoughts, the better you become at specifying what you feel.

It's clear that anger doesn't feel good. When we are angry our boundaries have been crossed, usually, and we are tense, often in the stomach. Think about it—remember when I said, "trust your gut?" When you get angry, your boundaries were crossed, likely in a situation that you could have predicted, but didn't because you didn't trust yourself enough to listen to your intuition. So you hold your anger in your gut.

It's easy to use the negative emotions when talking about our energy. What about the positive emotions? What does that feel like?

I'd like to say it feels calm and peaceful, and while, for the most part, that is true, we can be overly positive, in which case we go into a state of hyper-energy. This, too, does not benefit us. Have you ever felt so over-the-top energetic that your thoughts were racing and you couldn't get anything done because you couldn't focus? Likely, there is a reason for it. Our bodies, and in that I mean our physical bodies as well as our energy bodies, want to be in a state of balance. Yin and yang. Positive and negative, without having the intense extremes of either one. So, by tuning into yourself and understanding your emotions, you begin to understand your energy. Then you can make the changes you need to so that you can feel your power and own your freedom.

Love yourself!

CHAPTER 9

Who Are You?

DEAR SELF,

Why does everyone keep asking me if I know who I am? I know my name. I know what I do for a living. It's funny because, even though I know the answer, I can't help but shake the feeling that, perhaps there is more to the answer because it really does not seem like I know who I am anymore. What the heck does this question even mean? What's the correct answer? Am I looking for a different vocation or past time? More importantly, how do I even start the process of figuring it out?

One thing is for sure...I am not happy with where things are right now, and I feel like there is more out there. So maybe it's time to figure this out. I want to be happy, and I deserve that. Are you up for the adventure?

Love,
Yourself

AT THE CORE OF YOU, WHO ARE YOU? This took me a long time to answer. It's a big question. It defines everything you embody in this lifetime. There is no simple answer. Growing up, I used to think I had to define myself in terms of things, or in terms of career, or in terms of functionality (i.e. wife, mother, etc.). The healing process taught me that there really is no one-line answer for this question. It's complicated. We are complex creatures, after all. It doesn't make sense that our definition should be simplistic.

The other day, I realized the irony of "our core."

At the gym, we work hard to develop core strength. Everyone wants that six-pack. It's an accomplishment people marvel at. Magazine covers are dedicated to the washboard stomach, beach-ready bodies. Don't get me wrong. It IS an accomplishment. It takes work to achieve that. Real effort and dedication. When done appropriately, it lends itself to a healthy lifestyle, leaving us feeling great, in addition to looking great. Nonetheless, I sat there considering how ironic it is.

We focus on core strength in the gym, making that decision to dedicate time, energy, and resources to create an external version of ourselves that we believe is acceptable to the world.

Yet, when it comes to doing the inner work, there is this resistance. We are scared to death. Regardless of the level of determination or effort, going inward, looking at the core of who we are, is scary. You can never be too sure what skeletons might pop up, requiring us to face and deal with the things that still linger underneath the surface.

To be honest, though, the only way to truly heal is to let these skeletons show up, so you can process the events from a new perspective. More than likely, these events are multidimensional. It's not as simple as "someone did _____to you and now you feel _____."

It's like peeling back the layers of an onion. Just when you think you've healed from the event, you're reminded of another aspect of the situation that upset you or caused pain, and the process starts all over again. Perhaps this is why there isn't as much emphasis on us figuring out who we are at the core of our being. That takes real work and dedication to figure out. Interestingly, though, emotional healing lends itself to feeling great, and by extension, standing tall and looking great.

At some point along the healing journey, you might find yourself having what seems like an identity crisis. I know I did. I had to let go of much of what wasn't working. That created a space to call in something new, something better. I didn't know for myself what that was, exactly; I just knew there was "something." I found myself very confused, though, questioning...

Who am I?

I started with the obvious. My name. What I did for a living. I identified as a mother, a wife, a baker, a daughter, a friend, a business owner. These were very surface-level things, easy to identify, but not quite getting down to business. At my core, I knew that a few of these weren't really working anyway. In order to answer the question, you have to go a bit deeper, acknowledging both the positive AND the negative aspects of yourself and how you are showing up. This, my friends, can be a shocking and awakening moment.

I also started to look at my life in terms of what I did NOT want to identify as. A victim with low self-esteem; I could be controlling and even mean at times. I started to recognize situations where I acted out of judgement and fear, which caused me to be a little manipulative. These were not my proudest moments, but the more I looked back at my life, and let go of the situations that created so much pain, the more I discovered that it was easier to let go of the identities I did not want. I began to realize that there was more to me than I realized. In order to answer the question of identity, we need to acknowledge both the positive and negative aspects of our personalities. It was not a simple, black and white answer, but when you are totally honest with yourself about this, you can also take responsibility for your choices and actions. You decide how you want to show up and who you want to be. The situations don't decide for you. We don't have to identify as a victim or a martyr. We get to choose our response to any situation.

Maybe you aren't sure what that is exactly. You start questioning who you are. Believe me when I say this...this is a good sign (even though you might be thinking otherwise)! If you are questioning this, it means that you feel the call, that nudge, to contribute something greater to the Universe. It's a sign that you are shedding the fear, and ready to wake up and live. Think of it this way...fear is not present-focused, it's future-focused. If we are afraid, we are looking for what's next. If you are living in the present moment, you can monitor your thoughts, feelings, and actions in this moment, and then redirect, if needed. In the moment, there is no trauma—you know if you are safe, or happy, or tired. And you can do something about it. There's no need to fear.

If you've hit this point, you are ready to rediscover yourself. Redefine your life, on your terms, and according to your rules and expectations. Love yourself enough to become your own creation story. Recognize that you can define this any way that you want, and that there are many facets to the answer to this question. It depends on the day, the situation, those you are spending time with, and your mood. You are complex. There is no one, single, right adjective that can be the all-encompassing description to define who you are.

How exciting and miraculous and powerful that is!

Love yourself!

CHAPTER 10

Self-Love

DEAR SELF,

All I can say today is: isn't it time to show some love where love is due?

Haven't we been through enough? Enough pressure? Enough pain? Anxiety? Depression?

When do we get to feel the love that we give to everyone else?

Today! Today is the day! Because you are awesome and wonderful and amazing. And you deserve to feel that way. And to live a life that screams that.

It's time.

Love,
    Yourself

WHAT DOES SELF-LOVE MEAN TO YOU? Over the years, my definition has evolved considerably. I used to think that self-love involved manicures, massages, and naps on a Sunday afternoon. Don't get me wrong. These are all important aspects of self-love. They make you feel good and allow you to rest and recharge.

But self-love is also so much more!

When you love yourself, you make a conscious decision to do whatever is in your best interest to make yourself happy, healthy, and living an authentic life. It's not hard, but it is, truly, a conscious choice and requires effort. You come to this decision solely to benefit your own health, happiness, and wellbeing. Ultimately, we as individuals, are the only thing we have total control over in this lifetime. As hard as we might try, and as much as we might want to, we cannot control whether another individual chooses happiness and joy or pain and darkness, no matter how hard we love them. It's a difficult situation to watch. When you love someone and know they could be making better choices for their life, but they still decide to choose something entirely different, it can tear you up inside. It might even cause some tension or arguments between the two of you. Then, neither of you are happy.

So, in all reality, the only thing you can control is yourself. You might as well choose happiness for you, and then do the work that you need to do to create that for your life. You deserve to be happy. You deserve to wake up every single day and feel inspired and excited for the day ahead.

Life's not always rainbows and sunshine, but when you are a mindset where you love yourself, truly, you are much better equipped to get through the stormy days with a bit more ease and grace. When you have a strong love for yourself, you show up each day, courageously, honoring and accepting yourself, just as you are.

And do you wanna know something else?

When you are in that space for yourself, you also extend a little more grace to others. That love that you have for yourself allows you to hold space for those who are in pain, in times when they need it most. It allows you to show up with a little more compassion, and a greater capacity for understanding and forgiveness. (Note: that does not mean you allow yourself to be treated with disrespect.)

So, love yourself! And love yourself hard!

How do we do this? Let's break it down.

Self-love means the following:

- Holding yourself accountable for the choices you make.

  As I write this, the word "integrity" keeps coming to mind. Do what you say, say what you mean, and when things don't go as planned, don't bail and don't throw anyone else under the bus. This is not always an easy choice to make, but it is, in fact, an act of self-love because you are standing up for what you believe in. You made a choice based on something that you believed in. Own that. It doesn't matter what anyone else thinks. Love yourself enough to stand up for the choices you make and accept the fall out as it comes. Honestly, we are all adults here, right? So that means, even if the situation does not go as planned, we are able to work things out (hopefully and usually) like an adult. That means we accept responsibility, and, when necessary, apologize.

- Taking action on things you know you want to do, or need to do, without waiting for the approval or assistance of another.

Nobody can live your life for you. So, stop waiting for others to approve of your decisions before you take action. You are fully capable of taking action. You are fully capable of making a choice. Love yourself enough to own that. Give yourself permission to take action.

I will admit, there are going to be times when, perhaps, you don't have the information you need. Maybe there is a skillset that you need to develop. If that's the case, open your mind to working with a coach or mentor who can help you get the information you need in the best way possible. That is a totally different scenario. You are not asking that mentor for permission to act; rather, you are asking them to share their expertise so you can move forward. That is progress.

Be mindful and wary of unsolicited advice. Sometimes, people want to help. Other times, they cannot help themselves from inserting their opinion where it does not belong. We will give them the grace to express themselves, but we choose whether to accept their advice or not. I bring this up, mainly, for those looking to start a business in mind. Once you start talking to friends and family about your idea, they are going to try to tell you how to run your business, as if they know your product or service better than you do. You do not need to accept their advice. Honestly, you don't even have to listen to it, really. But how you handle the conversation is entirely up to you. If listening to their opinions saves you from the discomfort of an awkward or hostile holiday dinner, then it might be worthwhile listening. If you feel they are open to you saying, "hey, thanks, but I have this under control," then tell them. Either way, my point is—trust yourself and be ready to separate your wants, wishes, and desires from that of another person. It's your big idea. Own it. Don't be afraid to do it your way.

On the flip side, be able to accept if your idea needs tweaking. Be humble enough to say, "something is not working, what can I do to shift this so it improves?" Sometimes, that will require the advice from another. But do not squash your own intuition on the subject before you have had the opportunity to test your own ideas.

- Creating more space for you to breathe, relax, and play, in ways that benefit and uplift you.

Are you getting enough playtime these days? I think we forget that grownups need playtime, too. This is where those massages, pedicures, manicures, and peaceful Sunday afternoon naps come into play.

Is there a class you have always wanted to take? Something you have wanted to learn just for fun? Do it.

Do you want to set aside thirty minutes a day to read or write or play music? Get to it!

Is there a park you want to visit? Go!

When you take the time to get out and do the things that make you happy, like invest the time in a hobby, you give your brain a little bit of distance from the normal hustle of life. It's like hitting a reset button and it works like magic. Give yourself an hour of play, even just once a week. You will start to appreciate the other work that you do more. You will walk around feeling happier with yourself. And you will appreciate the other people around you, too, all because you are allowing yourself the time and space to do something solely for yourself.

- Setting and upholding boundaries.

I admit, this is probably the most challenging one on this entire list. I have an entire section on boundaries written in this book, they are that important.

Boundaries separate you from another. You get to decide what boundaries are established or yourself, and how you uphold them. You also get to choose the consequences when someone crosses your boundary.

- Nourishing yourself—mind, body, and soul—with sunshine, exercise, plenty of rest and water, and healthy foods.

It can be easy to underestimate the power of creating a mindfulness practice. What we put into our bodies, and what we feed our minds, impacts our energy. It affects how much or little we can create in a day, and who and what we are able to create time and space for. If we don't have the proper mindset, it makes it really challenging to get anything done, especially the things that we truly want to do.

Processed foods zap our energy. They are hard to digest and lack any real nutrients that we need to sustain energy levels. I am, in no way, advocating giving up your favorite snacks or sweets, but everything in moderation. Recognize that a healthy diet does not consist solely of cupcakes and potato chips. Listen to your body and give it what it needs when it's asking for it.

We need sunshine and fresh air. The sun, like a good night's rest, can recharge us on one of the more challenging days. Even a ten-minute walk in nature can help us clear our mind and continue with a task or project with a fresh and clear mind.

- Drink water.

- What type of music are you listening to? Is the music positive and inspiring to you?

- Are you taking time to read and nourish your brain?

What about meditation? Even taking five minutes out of your day to sit and just breathe can make a huge difference in mindset and attitude and energy. Observe your thoughts, without judgement, and with that awareness you can then start to notice what you say to yourself and make changes from there.

- Surrounding yourself with positive people who can support and uplift you when you need it, and you can do the same for them.

I used to hate hearing the phrase "find your tribe" or "your tribe affects your vibe" but you know what? They are true. We are social beings. We need to be around people. And if you are on a mission to accomplish anything in life, spend your time with people who can support you in that mission. Those who are not on board will try to hold you back. They will take every opportunity to cross your boundaries, and it takes a lot of energy for you to have to remind them that you have those boundaries in the first place. On the other hand, we need people in our corner who can be our cheerleader when we need it, and who believe in our mission and purpose, so that on days when we might not believe in ourselves, they remind us what it is we are working towards.

Ultimately, it's great if you can include people who motivate you to keep growing, those who might be ten steps ahead of you. These are the people who will inspire you, because you can look to them to see what could be coming down the road for you, if you just worked a teeny, tiny bit more.

These are not always easy to do. Sometimes you have to make choices you never imagined you'd have to make. Sometimes this involves letting people go from your life. You might even experience resistance from other people, particularly when you start to uphold your own boundaries.

Love yourself anyway!

When you do, the light within you gets brighter, and shines out into the world. That, my friends, is precisely what the world needs. You! No matter how many other people out there are doing something similar to what you currently do, or want to do in the future, they are not you. They do not bring your expertise, energy, or energy, or your own unique voice. When we show up every single day, loving ourselves, we are more inclined to share ourselves with the world. And each unique perspective, when shared in a manner that supports the rest of humanity, lifts other people up to also show up as their best selves. It's an amazing cycle of life that begins and ends with one person. You! Love yourself. When you do, you light the rest of the world up, too, inspiring other people to also love and nurture themselves to be their best self.

One tiny spark ignites the entire flame. That tiny spark is you! Do you see how powerful you are?

Love yourself!

CHAPTER 11

On the Other Side

DEAR SELF,

When are we going to stop and ask: "when is life going to change?" When is it time to realize that we deserve more? That we are enough?

Isn't it time?

Love,
  Yourself

YOU ARE WORTHY AND YOU ARE ENOUGH!

Did you hear that? How does that feel?

- Did you get that warm-and-fuzzy, happy feeling that leaves you smiling from ear-to-ear, so much so that you can almost feel yourself glow and shine from the inside out?
- ...or did you feel a tightness, almost like a knot in your stomach that makes you want to run and hide under a rock?

Have you ever thought to yourself?:

- "Enough already, I am healed, I swear!"
- ...or you feel yourself rolling your eyes every time you hear someone mention healing and overcoming trauma
- ...or maybe you think to yourself "hey I am doing the work, but am not getting anywhere, and so this healing stuff is probably just a bunch of crap anyway"...?

In all honesty, not long ago, I was telling myself the same thing. I had started this journey a few years before, and I thought that it was coming to an end. Basically, I thought I had figured my shit out, and was waiting for that magical moment when life would be all sunshine and rainbows, and I would have everything I could have ever wanted and hoped for. I just needed to heal a little bit more before it happened. Little did I know - I had no idea. I didn't know what I didn't know. And what I didn't know was that I was stuck. Still. Stuck. Or so I thought.

Three years of work! Of understanding energy. Of understanding limiting beliefs. Of trying to make a change. Three years of one step forward and ten steps back. Three years going down this road of healing and awakening, and here I was, stuck. I was frustrated! I had been trying to get my life together. I THOUGHT I finally "got it". Yet here I was, at a point, yet again, where I found myself stuck. Much like the day I found myself sobbing on the side of a mountain, crying in fear for my life, here I was, again, only this time, I was safe at home, sobbing in my bed, and thinking "what. the. fuck. just. happened."

I felt such tremendous pain all over my body. That day, I hurt. Bad! I tried to blame everyone else around me in that moment...

- Maybe that person (the other party in this situation) caused this---because she misled me and lied to me and clearly, she is a terrible person and needs to get her life together.
- Maybe it was my parents---because some of it probably was, and that always seems like an easy out anyway.
- Maybe it was that coach I hired---because it was her job to fix me - that was what I was paying her to do, and here I was still in emotional pain and stuck.
- Maybe it was my ex-husband's fault---because he never loved me and spent so many years abusing me and my kids.
- Maybe...maybe...maybe...

Then, I had a realization...this moment of total clarity, and brutal honesty, with myself--perhaps for the first time in forever. Sitting on my bed, crying, and thinking about what just happened, there was only one conclusion I could come to that actually made any sense...

I was, and am, 100% responsible!

Looking at the situation that just occurred, there was nobody else to blame but myself. I had no choice but take responsibility. Because, ultimately, I saw the red flags. I knew there was going to be an issue. I felt it. I had even predicted it in my mind, even though I would never have admitted that out loud to anyone at the time. I just didn't trust it! So, in that moment, I was the problem! Nobody else! ME!

There is nothing quite like having one of those "oh shit" moments in life slap you right in the face.

Looking at the situation that just occurred, there was nobody else to blame but myself. I had no choice but take responsibility. Because, ultimately, I saw the red flags. I knew there was going to be an issue. I felt it. I had even predicted it in my mind, even though I would never have admitted that out loud to anyone at the time. I just didn't trust it! So, in that moment, I was the problem! Nobody else! ME!

There is nothing quite like having one of those "oh shit" moments in life slap you right in the face.

I started to have these flashes from my past; times when things went wrong, and I blamed other people. I tried to control and blame, point the finger, judge and get angry, usually throwing me into a moment where I looked and sounded like I was totally out of control. Back then, it seemed okay -- because *they* did it to me first. It was *their* fault for making me angry. Their fault, because what they did was wrong, or bad. Then I realized - I didn't have to react so poorly. I could have chosen to smile and be loving. I could have chosen to seek to understand. I could have chosen to just walk away.

In that moment, I realized, in a completely new and totally powerful way, that I was, and am, 100% responsible for my life. For myself. For my thoughts, feelings, beliefs, behavior. What I do. What I say. How I feel...all me! And this happened *after* I had already done some work through my healing.

Let me be clear. I am NOT saying that what they did was okay. A shitty move is still a shitty move.

In my mind, though, there is a code that governs how people should be treated. That code also applies to me! And the truth is: the only person responsible for making me follow that code, is me. That means that I get to choose if I treat people with respect and kindness or treat them like dirt. I get to choose if I fly off the handle in a fit of rage, or if I walk away. I get to choose to lie or tell the truth. I get to choose!

I am 100% responsible for my life and how I show up in this world!

Until I got this lesson, until I truly, and wholeheartedly GOT IT, I would remain stuck. It didn't matter how many affirmations I tried to write, or how often I tried to write my gratitude list. It didn't matter how much I tried to manifest. I had to accept 100% responsibility for my life and my actions and my beliefs, and I had to realize that that came down to the power within me to choose what I wanted for my life. Exercising that power to choose gave me strength. Courage. Clarity. And I could finally see that, by accepting responsibility, I was no longer a victim. I didn't have to stay stuck. I could create new habits, new beliefs, new systems for living my life that allowed me to be happy.

And here's the thing -- accepting this truth came down to one understanding...I am enough, and I am worthy!

If you are anything like me, the first time I told myself "I am enough, and I am worthy" I felt such a tightness in the pit of my stomach. I didn't believe it. I didn't feel it. And I wasn't living it either.

But there was one thing that I did feel, know, and believe. I got to choose! I didn't have to choose to stay there. I decided to choose something different. I chose to pivot. I chose to create change. My way. For me.

I didn't have all the answers, but what I did know was:
I am 100% responsible for my life.
I wasn't happy with where I was or how I felt.
I wanted more out of life, and I wanted to feel like I was enough.

What I had been doing was not working. It was time for something new. This was a process. It did not happen overnight (insert image of Bambi trying to walk for the first time here).

New behaviors and actions. That was the start. I gave myself a new routine. This was a challenge at first. After all those years of living how I was, I was afraid of what life would look like on the other side. That fear allowed me to let in distractions. Then, I realized, I was changing, but my reasons weren't strong enough. Up until that point, I thought I knew why I was doing it, then I realized I wasn't really in alignment with what I was saying I wanted. My actions and effort didn't match that. I had to re-frame my why. Then I had to re-frame my actions and effort.

It was a process. It took time. It took effort. And, yes, it's still evolving. Even now!

Once you get yourself into this habit of awareness for your life, and you allow yourself to take those baby steps, you create the momentum you need. You build credibility with yourself. Guess what? Eventually, you start to believe. In that belief, it becomes easier to recognize when things aren't working, when you need to pivot and make another new choice.

The truth is-- there really is no "other side" of healing. We are never truly "healed." Yes, we can show up and look at our lives, and we can forgive and let go. And then we are going to get new lessons, which brings new opportunities for more healing and growth. It does not stop. We are always healing. Healing is not the final destination before your life begins. Eventually, though, you will wake up one day and realize that, even though you don't have all the answers--your life isn't perfect, and you don't have everything figured out--THAT IS OKAY!

No matter what, it does not change the fact that you are enough, and you are worth it - no matter what that "it" is. You are 100% responsible for making it happen or choosing not to.

So, if you are anything like I was, stop waiting to be healed for your life to start. Start right now! With that awareness and understanding, you can start to look at your life in a new way. Decide what actions you need to stop, and which ones you need to start, so that you can allow your life to truly begin. Because you are enough, and you are worth it!

And with that, one day you wake up and realize that life looks different. Something has changed. There is peace. Stillness in the midst of the actions of life. YOU have changed. You chose you, and now you can live your life from that place of authentic gratitude, happiness, and joy, realizing that you don't have it all figured out, but you are on your way to evolving.

Love yourself!

CHAPTER 12

Surrender and Reflection

DEAR SELF,

Broken, beaten. Completely torn down.

Feeling every emotion, every pain, every sadness, every fear, and every dagger that has been pierced through my heart.

The pain is so intense, all I can think is "please, God, take me now."

Trying to cut through the rubble of my life before me, deciding what is mine and what is not.

What belongs to me? Which emotions? Which are thoughts, beliefs, feelings of others? And which do I keep and which do I let fall away? It's a choice I must make now...

Continue carrying the weight of the world on, in, and around me, allowing it to define and shape my existence?

Or

Surrender. Let go. Release. Pivot!

Love,
Yourself

Now, it's time to dig in, surrender, and get to work.

Here, I have listed some questions that you can use to reflect, a guide to your own healing journey. If you have already started the healing process, perhaps these questions will give you insight into a theme in your life that you have already been working through or it will show you an area that you had not considered. If you are new to the healing process, these questions can be a starting point.

There is no right or wrong way to go about this journey. Answer the questions all at once, or one at a time. The important thing is to do it. Get started. Put yourself in motion, with the intention that you are going to create the change in your life that you deserve and want. Then, choose to commit to yourself that you will be completely honest with yourself as you answer these questions, and will answer them fully and completely. Sometimes this means you have to answer the question, then go back to it at a later point to decide if there's more you want and need to say.

Don't be surprised if topics and situations from your life come back up multiple times. As you move through the healing process, you are peeling back the layers of your heart, your mind, your body, and your soul. It's a multidimensional process. With new levels of awareness, you can then return to situations that you previously believed were healed, and see it from a deeper perspective, allowing yourself to heal another dimension of that situation.

Manage your energy as you go through this. This process takes time and energy. Your ego is likely to resist this process for a little while. That is okay. Take a rest when you need it, even if you have to put this on hold for a few days but set the intention that you are not going to quit.

Be mindful of how your body feels through this process. Where in your body do you feel the emotions? For me, I felt it most in my heart and my stomach. This information gave me clues to connect with physical symptoms I was experiencing, after the doctors had told me there was nothing wrong with me.

Stay open to finding the lessons. Remain open and present to what you feel. Remember, you have to feel it to heal it. Don't judge the situation or your feelings about it. This creates resistance. Allow your feelings to come up, so that you can let them go. This creates the flow that you need to move all the negative feelings up and out of you.

Lastly, do not be afraid to ask for help, guidance, and support as you go through this. Find a coach, mentor, guide, therapist who can help you. Or, give this book to a friend and take the journey together to support one another. It is easier to move mountains when the tribe is there to help. You do not have to take this journey alone.

Okay, so grab a notebook, a pen, and a box of tissues, and let's get going!

Love yourself!

Reflection Questions

- How do you describe yourself? Why? Do you think others describe you that way? Why?
- What are your skills and talents? Are you using these on a regular basis now? If so, how does that feel? If not, why not?
- When you meet someone new, what do you tell them? How do you introduce yourself? How does that story make you feel?
- What story do you want to be able to tell someone about your life? What version of the story will make you feel proud that it is authentically yours?
- What challenges do you feel you are facing in life right now? If you could wave a magic wand, what would you change? How do you feel waking up each day and how would you prefer to feel instead?
- Do you say what you mean? Do you do what you say? Are you creating misunderstandings within yourself, and with others, by not following through and honoring yourself in this manner? How?
- What people, places, or situations make you feel the most triggered? By this, I mean what makes you uncomfortable, angry, or frustrated? Are there common themes? Examine each situation or each relationship that you list. Sit for a few minutes and really question why. What is it about that that stirs up so much angst? Ask yourself "what lessons need to be learned from this?"
- Are you willing to take a stand on things you believe in? Are you willing to share your thoughts and opinions with others, without fear of judgement? If so, how does that feel? If not, why? What holds you back?
- Who or what inspires you and why?
- Whom do you need to forgive? Why? Are you ready to?

- Who has acknowledged you for your accomplishments, skills, or abilities? How did it feel to receive this acknowledgement?
- What do you believe about love? Do you love yourself? How do you show it? How are you showing and accepting love from others? Who taught you about love? What was the message you received from them?
- Do you tell the truth in all situations without blame or judgement?
- As a child, how did you spend your time? What did you do for fun? How are you spending your time now? Do you take time to laugh and play? What would it mean for you to do that? How would it feel?
- What is it that you would like to create? What do you feel is holding you back from creating it? How would it feel for you to bring that creation to life?
- What does self-love mean to you? How does it feel to take time for yourself and honor yourself?
- What skills do you want to acquire and why?
- What will be different in your life when you begin to love yourself? What is holding you back?
- Was there ever a time in your life where you showed yourself love consistently? How did that feel? Why did that stop?
- What is the first memory of you feeling rejection or sadness? What did that experience teach you? Is that lesson something that you want to hold onto now?
- What does personal freedom mean to you?

CHAPTER 13

Writing Your Own Love Letters

ON THE PAGES THAT FOLLOW, you will find the beginning of several love letters that you can write to yourself. Use the space provided or start an entry in your journal using these as prompts. Don't worry about spelling or punctuation or grammar. The goal is to allow yourself to celebrate some of your wins, to feel proud of who you are right now, and to see that you are amazing. It is one hundred percent okay to feel proud of what you have accomplished, or to feel inspired by something that brings you joy, or to feel gratitude for anything, big or little, that you have in your life right now.

As with the suggestion to go through the reflection questions with a friend, you can also use these letters to lift someone else in your life who might need it.

But guess what? The more you start to allow yourself to sit with these feelings, and notice all of your successes, the easier it becomes to know, see, feel, and believe in your awesome-ness. When this happens, you will truly take inspired action in your life. You will trust yourself enough to listen to your intuition. You will have set boundaries. You will treat yourself well, honoring and trusting that, whatever it is you want to create in this world is beautiful and valuable, and necessary—for you and for those who will benefit from your unique abilities and talents. You will recognize that there is no one set "right way" or "guaranteed method" of anything—success and fulfillment included. The only surefire path to achieve happiness is by sitting down, tuning in, and listening, truly listening, to your own heart.

Love yourself!

DEAR YOU,

Good morning, beautiful! Today is going to be an amazing day because...

Don't forget to shine!

Love,
  Yourself

DEAR SELF,
Here is how I intend to shine today...

I totally got this!

Love,
    Yourself

DEAR YOU,
I am so freaking proud of you today because...

Love,
   Yourself

DEAR YOU,

Remember that day when we felt so strong and capable? Let's take a minute to reflect on the details of that bad-ass day. I remember that...

Way to go! (insert happy dance here)

Love,

Yourself

DEAR SELF,

As a kid, I always loved to...

And here's why...

It would be amazing to spend some time doing that again!
Let's get it on the calendar!

Love,

Yourself

DEAR YOU,

Today was NOT the most stellar of days. Here's why...

And now I feel...

But that's okay! Here is what I can learn from it...

And here is what I need to do right now in order to reset myself back to feeling like me...

Way to go today! It might not have been easy, but we got through it! See how strong we are!

Love,

Yourself

DEAR SELF,

What is going on? Why do I feel so off balance lately? What has changed? What do I need to recognize and focus on?

I can totally do this!

Love,

Yourself

DEAR SELF,

Right here and now, the top 10 things I am grateful for are:

Life is good!

Love,

Yourself

DEAR SELF,

My top 5 proudest moments in life include...

See! I can do it!

Love,

Yourself

DEAR SELF,

Looking back, if I could tell my teenage self anything, I would say the following:

Woah! Look at how far we've come!

Love,
    Yourself

ABOUT THE AUTHOR

Author Elizabeth Miles is a certified life and business coach, and founder of Healing Lotus Connection, a company dedicated to helping others connect to themselves, to their hearts, as a pathway to discovering their purpose in life. Her first book *This Is Where You Pivot: This Shift from Fear to Freedom* was published in 2019. She is also a speaker and the co-founder of the youth leadership series The Recipe for Leadership Project, designed to teach kids about communication, mindset, and taking leadership of their own lives. Elizabeth obtained her bachelor's degree in psychology as well as her Master of Business Administration, and a diploma in baking and pastry. Elizabeth is a Philadelphia local, mom of four, animal lover, and loves reading, writing, and music. Connect with Elizabeth online via Facebook (@HealingLotusConnection) or on Instagram (@healingconnectionpa). #powertopivot

This Is Where You Pivot: The Shift from Fear to Freedom
- Published July 2019
- No matter where you are on your journey, we are never stuck, lost, or alone. At any given moment, we can use our #powertopivot, make a new choice, and start again. Join Elizabeth in this conversation as she shares her experiences overcoming trauma, weight issues, and depression, and learn how she pivoted to a mindset that set her on a path to freedom and fulfillment.

Coming Soon:
The Power to Pivot Workbook Series, Workbook 1:
- Coming September 2020